# YORK
## A-Z

J. Pine's engraving in Francis Drake's *Eboracum*. It depicts five putti salvaging books and manuscripts from the all consuming clutches of Father Time and storing them in an ancient urn. The Latin reads 'Nor shall antiquity consume the past records of your homeland', in other words, historians must keep on rescuing the past from oblivion – nowhere is that more apposite than in a city like York.

# YORK
## A-Z

## PAUL CHRYSTAL

*Foreword by Keith Hyman,*
*Lord Mayor of York*

*2012-2013*

FONTHILL

*'Beware how you destroy your antiquities, guard them with religious care! They are what give you a decided character and superiority over other provincial cities. You have lost much, take care of what remains.'*

William Etty 1787-1849

*Front cover:* York Minster in 2013 from the Marks & Spencer building in Parliament Street (main picture); York Railway Station *c.* 1910, courtesy of Melvyn Browne; Bootham Bar and the Minster, from *Historic York – 34 Water Color Facsimiles of England's Most Picturesque City* by J. S. Fletcher, published by the Photochrom Co Ltd, London & Detroit; Millenium Bridge, 2013.

*Back Cover:* York Royal Station Hotel with the Yorkshire Wheel in 2013; The Bar Walls *c.* 1912.

Fonthill Media Limited
Fonthill Media LLC
www.fonthillmedia.com
office@fonthillmedia.com

Published in 2013

British Library Cataloguing in Publication Data:
A catalogue record for this book is available from the British Library

Copyright © Paul Chrystal, 2013

ISBN 978-1-78155-291-9

Typeset in 10pt on 13pt Sabon LT
Printed and bound in England

Connect with us
 facebook.com/fonthillmedia twitter.com/fonthillmedia

# Introduction

2012 was a significant year for the City of York. It was 800 years since King John granted a Royal Charter in 1212 allowing the city political self-determination and trading practices controlled by the guilds. How the citizens of York deployed these rights has shaped and influenced York's history and heritage to this day. *York A-Z* has been published one year after this important anniversary to coincide with a year long programme of events celebrating York's status as a city. Residents and visitors came together to enjoy the Mystery Plays, a Festival of the Rivers, York Chocolate Festival, Railfest, and a whole host of other activities redolent of York's past 800 years.

The significance of these events, and hundreds of others is revealed in *York A-Z* – a manageable and convenient survey of the city's history which can be read from A to Z or dipped into at leisure.

In 1920 George VI, then Duke of York, received the freedom of the city and said that the 'history of York is the history of England'. Even allowing for regal hyperbole his observation confirms just how rich, deep and extensive the history of York is. If it does not match precisely the history of our nation then York's history and heritage certainly reflects and informs it in many different ways. This book will help to show how it does that, informing and entertaining visitor and resident alike.

Paul Chrystal,
York, August 2013

# About the Author

Paul Chrystal is author of more than twenty–five books covering the history of York and Yorkshire; ancient Rome ; the history of chocolate and confectionery, the history of tea, coffee and cocoa; the Rowntree family; and lifeboat stations of the north east.

As well as being author and historian, Paul was a medical publisher for over thirty years; he now writes for national newspapers and appears regularly on BBC local radio and on the BBC World Service.

# Acknowledgements

My thanks to Melvyn Browne for permission to use a number of postcards and pictures throughout the book; and to John Roden for permission to use the photograph on page 90 originally published in his *The Minster School, York: A Centenary History 1903-2004*. Thanks too go to Keith and Karen Hyman, Lord Mayor and Lady Mayoress of York, 2012-2013 for their support and encouragement.

Text in **bold type** within an entry signifies a main entry.

# Foreword

2012 marked 800 years since the City of York was granted a Royal Charter allowing it to elect a Lord Mayor to govern the affairs of its residents; this then is an appropriate time to publish a book that helps to show some of the history of this remarkable city.

Over the years the role of mayor has changed and the present Lord Mayors take on the responsibility for only one year and must be a serving Councillor. This contrasts with some of York's earlier holders of the title who were in place for as long as eighteen years giving them unprecedented power over trade and commercial development. There has also been several famous and interesting characters in the past such as members of the Rowntree and Terry families, the famous railway barons Hudson and Leeman and the architect John Carr. Then there was Lord Mayor Agar who was stabbed by a drunken sailor in 1618. Luckily this type of incident is rare and no recent holder of the title has upset the residents so much.

To mark the 800th year of its Royal Charter in 2012, York held many events, a number of which stand out: the Olympic Flame was in York in June and the Paralympic torch in August; the Mystery Plays made a welcome return and in April the Queen visited the City to distribute the Royal Maundy Money in a service at York's great church, the Minster. As 2012 was her Diamond Jubilee year this is a great honour for the City of York.

I hope that *York A-Z* will help you to understand more about the history of York and that you will then appreciate even more what a great place it is.

Keith Hyman,
Lord Mayor of York, 2012-2013

A full list of all the Mayors of York can be found at www. mansionhouseyork.com

John Speed's 1610 map of York.

# The A to Z

## 800

York 800 was a year long series of events and festivities in 2012 marking the 800th anniversary of King John's charter in 1212 conferring city status on York. Before then the city, indeed the whole County of Yorkshire, was governed by the Sheriff from York **Castle**. The fact that he was not accountable caused resentment amongst traders and citizens who demanded a bigger say in how the city was run. In 1155 Henry II granted the first charter (signed by Thomas Becket) allowing the city its liberties and laws and exemption from lestage taxes (duties payable on unlading in port). Three years before signing the *Magna Carta* in 1215 King John extended this by giving the city the opportunity to buy the right to govern themselves. John's charter permitted York's citizens, in the guise of **Freemen** of the city , not the Sheriff, to collect and pay taxes to the Crown, and to appoint a **Lord Mayor**. Henry III went a step further when he granted charters relating to the administration of law and justice. The Sheriff was, as a result, powerless. From then on, until 1974, York was a municipal democracy operating under its own Mayors. In 1377 the population was 13,500 – a third of London's and the second largest in Britain; as regards **trade** York was the country's sixth biggest city. York was undisputedly England's second city.

## Alcuin

Alcuin (d. AD 804) spent most of his celebrated life in York and was master of the **Minster School.** He went on to teach at Charlemagne's palace in Aachen and is one of the founding fathers of European culture. He describes York in his *On the Saints of the Church of York*: '...My heart is set to praise my home And briefly tell the ancient cradling Of York's famed city through the charms of verse.' Alcuin's extensive library was one of the best and biggest in the world and helped York to become one of the premier seats of learning in the eighth century. Unfortunately, the **Vikings** destroyed much of the collection in 867.

## Aldwark

Old werks, or fortification. Home of the Merchant Taylor's Guild, **Jonathan Martin,** Minster arsonist and Hunt's Brewery until the 1950s.

## Alexander II, King of the Scots
Alexander married Margaret, second daughter of Henry III and Queen Eleanor of Provence in **York Minster** in 1251; the bride was eleven, the groom ten. Alexander went on to rule the Scots through a golden age of Scottish history.

## Alexander, William
One of York's earliest **booksellers** and **printers;** he refused to publish novels, considering them far too ephemeral. His self-censorship was to cost him dearly, if this story is to be believed. Walter Scott, while researching *Ivanhoe,* came to York and visited Alexander's bookshop where he suggested Alexander might publish his book. Alexander declined, saying, 'I esteem your friendship but I fear thy books are too worldly for me to print'. He paid for his rebuff, though, as the bookseller is thought to be the boring Dr Dryasdust to whom Scott dedicated *Ivanhoe*. In 1796 he married Anne Tuke, daughter of **William Tuke.**

## All Saints, North Street
A stunning church by any standard; it comprises Early English, Decorated and Perpendicular styles and features an octagonal tower with an unusual 120' spire. Emma Raughton, a visionary anchorite, lived in an anchorhold here – a two-storey house attached to the aisle. The church has some of the finest mediaeval stained glass in Europe not in York Minster, including the aisle window which shows the Six Corporal Acts of Mercy (as in Matthew's Gospel) and the famous 1410 Doom Window (or **'Pricke of Conscience'** window) which graphically depicts your last fifteen days before the Day of Judgement. There is also an outstanding fifteenth-century hammer-beam ceiling decorated with beautiful, colourful angels. Other treasures include a figure in one of the fourteenth-century windows wearing glasses – one of the earliest depictions of spectacles – and representations of the green man in the aisles and nave. Around 1500 York had eight monasteries and **friaries,** over forty parish churches and two ecclesiastical colleges.

## All Saints, Pavement
Notable for its fascinating lantern tower – a fifteenth-century beacon guiding travellers in to the city from the outlying areas, notably the dark and dangerous Forest of Galtres. The north door sanctuary knocker shows a lion devouring a sinner.

## Almshouses
The first recorded almshouse in Britain was founded by King Athelstan in York in the tenth century. Surviving York almshouses include Ingram's: a row of ten cottages in **Bootham;** they were built in 1632 by Sir Arthur Ingram for ten indigent widows. Their spiritual needs were met by a chapel with bell tower in the centre of the row of cottages; its doorway comprised a highly ornate Norman arch bought from Holy Trinity in Micklegate. Their endowment provided £5.00 each every year, a gown every three years and 'twenty nobles yearly to some honest and able man for reading prayers in the house'. Also in Bootham are Mary Wandesford's almshouses: in her 1725 will Mary Wandesford left a bequest to fund what is now Wandesford House, built around 1740;

it was known then as the 'Old Maids Hospital'. There is also **Dorothy Wilson's** School on Foss Bridge. Lady Hewley's almshouses, established in 1700, are on St Saviourgate set up by Lady Sarah Hewley (1627-1710); these discriminated in favour of religious 'dissenters', mainly **Unitarian** initially. The almshouses were originally in Tanner Row, but were relocated to accomodate York's second **railway station**. Other York almshouses include Margaret Mason's Hospital in Colliergate opened in 1732 for six poor widows, closing in 1958; and the **Terry** Memorial Homes and Ann Middleton's Hospital in Skeldergate. The hospital was paid for by an endowment from Dame Anne Middleton in 1659, the wife of Peter Middleton, Sheriff of York, and served as a refuge for twenty widows of the **Freemen** of the City of York. **St Thomas's Hospital** was in **Micklegate**.

## Ancient Society of York Florists
Established in 1768 the Society is the world's oldest horticultural society and runs the world's longest running flower show; it is now at Askham Bryan but before that was in Colliergate and at Baynes Coffee House in Petergate.

## Anderson, Tempest
Tempest Anderson (1846-1913) was an ophthalmic surgeon at York **County Hospital**; he was also an expert amateur photographer and volcanologist who witnessed the volcanic eruptions in the West Indies in 1902 and 1907. Born in York, he died on board ship in the Red Sea while returning from a trip to the volcanoes of Indonesia and the Philippines and is buried in Suez, Egypt. Tempest was President of the **Yorkshire Philosophical Society** in 1912 when he presented the Society with a 300-seat lecture theatre (the Tempest Anderson Hall) annexed to the **Yorkshire Museum**. His unrivalled photographic collection exceeds 3,000 images, many of which were taken during his travels.

## The Anglian Tower
An adjunct to the **Roman** walls in the Museum Gardens close to the **Multangular Tower**. Probably very late Roman, it comprises a tunnel vaulted square tower with arched doorways.

## Archbishop Holgate's School
The school is, after **St Peter's**, the oldest in York, and was founded as Archbishop Holgate's Grammar School in 1546 by Robert Holgate, financed by capital from the Dissolution of the Monasteries. The original grammar school was in Ogleforth and known as The Reverend Shackley's School; **Thomas Cooke** taught here, the famous optical instrument manufacturer who went on to establish T. Cooke & Sons, later **Cooke, Troughton & Simms** the equally famous telescope manufacturers. In 1858 the school merged with the Yeoman School when it moved to Lord Mayor's Walk; it relocated again in 1963 to its present site in Badger Hill. Chemistry teacher and old boys Albert Holderness and John Lambert are the authors of one of the most successful school chemistry books ever published: *School Certificate Chemistry* published in

1936; the 500,000<sup>th</sup> copy came off the press in 1962 and the book remains in print today in its sixth edition, retitled *A New Certificate Chemistry*. Archbishop Holgate was the first protestant **archbishop,** in 1545, and the first to marry. He deserted both his religion and his wife when the Catholic Mary Tudor acceded to the throne in 1553.

### Archbishop of York
The first Bishop of York was Paulinus in 625 – sent by Pope Gregory I to convert the Anglo Saxons to Christianity, one of whom was King Edwin of Northumbria; another was Hilda of Whitby. Egbert was the first Archbishop of York from 732 to 766. The current archbishop, the ninety-seventh, is the Most Reverend and Right Honourable Dr John Tucker Mugabi Sentamu, inaugurated in November 2005. Born in Uganda he became a barrister, antagonising Idi Amin; he came to Britain in 1974 and was Bishop of Birmingham from 2002; Dr Sentamu is Britain's first black archbishop.

### Aske, Robert
One of the leaders of the Pilgrimage of Grace who was hanged in chains from Clifford's Tower for his troubles by Henry VIII in 1537. He died a slow death a week later; his body was left there for a year as a warning to other potential traitors.

Inside the Assembly Rooms showing the original seating.From an engraving by W. Lindley in 1759 in York City Art Gallery entitled *A Perspective View of the Inside of the Grand Assembly Room in Blake Street, 1759*.

The Assembly Rooms in Blake Street, 1836. Etridge's Hotel is on the right, built around 1740 as Bluitt's Inn, and patronised by the King of Denmark in August 1768. It was demolished in 1859.

## Assembly Rooms
One of the earliest neo-classical buildings in Europe in Blake Street, the 1732 Assembly Rooms were designed by the Earl of Burlington in the Palladian style; they were paid for by subscription to provide the local gentry with somewhere sumptuous to play dice and cards, dance and drink tea, as featured in Smollett's *The Expedition of Humphrey Clinker*. The building epitomised the age of elegance and helped make York the capital of north country fashion – a northern Bath. The main hall is surrounded by forty-eight magnificent Corinthian pillars. Sedan chair men met in the cellars here; it was requisitioned by the Food Office in 1939. In 1751 the seats from the aisles were removed to the front of the columns for use by ladies with wide hooped skirts, too wide for them to pass between the columns, as pointed out by the Duchess of Marlborough. This was much to the disgust of Hermit in York who, in 1823, described them as fit only for 'the market women of Covent Garden'.

## The Astronomical Clock
From 1750 until 1871 the south entrance to the **Minster** was surmounted by a splendid clock. This was installed in 1750 by Henry Hindley to replace a ramshackle mediaeval clock. Henry Hindley's Striking Clock was moved to the North Transept where it features two carved oak figures or 'Quarter Jacks' who strike the hours and quarters with their rods. As famous today is the Astronomical Clock installed in the Minster

An 1844 photograph of the clock over the south door.

in 1955 as a memorial to the Yorkshire-based Allied aircrew who flew from bases in Yorkshire and the North-East and who died during the Second World War. One face shows the precise position of the sun in relation to the Minster at any given time while the other gives the position of the northern stars by which aircrew would have navigated.

## Auden, W. H.

Wystan Hugh Auden was born at number 54, **Bootham** on 21 February 1907; his father, G. A. Auden, was Medical Officer for York and author of *The Gild of Barber Surgeons of the City of York*.

## J. Backhouse & Son Ltd, Nurserymen

An early day, state-of-the-art garden centre run by Darlington **Quaker** James Backhouse in Fishergate with 'branches' in Acomb, Poppleton Road and Toft Green. They bought the gardens of George Telford, another celebrated gardener who, according to **Francis Drake** in *Eboracum* was 'one of the first that brought our northern gentry into the method of planting all kinds of forest trees, for use and ornament'. James and his brother Thomas were nationally celebrated nurserymen: their gardens were collectively called the *Kew of the North* . They were responsible for the cultivation of numerous rare plants, some of which James brought back from South Africa and Australasia. A particularly striking feature was a 25-feet-high Alpine gorge built with 400 tons of rock which led to a surge in rockeries all over the country. In 1938 the nurseries were sold to the Corporation who made them into a park; this lasted until 1946 when it was all covered over. Backhouse had been producing catalogues long before 1821 when the second edition of their pithily titled *Catalogue of Fruit & Forest Trees, Evergreen & Deciduous Shrubs, Ornamental Annual, Biennial Plants, also of Culinary, Officinal & Agricultural Plants* was published.

## The Baedeker Raid, 28 April 1942

The raids on York, Norwich, Bath, Canterbury and Exeter became known as Baedeker because Goring's staff allegedly used the famous travel guide to select their Vergeltungsangriffe (retaliatory) targets – namely 3 *** English cities – in retaliation for the RAF destruction of Lubeck and Rostock. Seventy German bombers, largely unopposed, bombed York for two hours: eighty-six people died including fourteen children, and ninety-eight were seriously injured (not including undisclosed army and RAF fatalities). 9,500 houses (30 per cent of the city's stock) were damaged or destroyed leaving 2,000 people homeless. **The Guildhall** and **St Martin le Grand Church** were badly damaged. **The Bar Convent School** collapsed killing five nuns including the

The Guildhall ablaze; photographs like these were suppressed until well after the war ended.

Death and destruction at the Bar Convent.

headmistress, Mother Vincent. The following day the *Daily Mail* reported: 'The gates of York still stand high, like the spirit of its people who, after nearly two hours of intense bombing and machine-gunning, were clearing up today'. There is a plaque on **York Railway Station** in honour of Station Foreman William Milner who died in the raid while entering a burning building to get medical supplies. His body was found still holding the box; he was posthumously awarded the King's Commendation for Gallantry.

## The Bagnio
The Northern Bagnio was down Leopard's Passage, opposite **St Martin's Church** in **Coney Street** and dates from 1691. The *London Gazette* of 19 October announces it as follows: 'Laconicum Boreale or the Northern Bagnio ... where all persons who desire the same may be admitted to sweat and bath; and be cup'd (if they please) after the German fashion ... paying 5s a piece'. By 1735 it had become Alexander Staples' printing office for the *York Courant*, later Ward's the Organ Builders, demolished in 1924.

## Baile Hill
The first of York's two castles built by William the Conqueror in 1068 and fortified with a timber fort; it soon became redundant but **Bitchdaughter Tower** here was used as an artillery emplacement in the Civil War.

Baile Hill is to the left of this fascinating 1911 shot of sheep in Cromwell Road.

## The Barber-Surgeons of York (Ebor)

The Barber-Surgeons of York (Ebor) were responsible for professional medical training and practitioner licensing in York until the establishment of the **York Medical Society** and York's first **medical school**. G. A. Auden, father of **WH Auden,** has done considerable research on the Gild. The first Barber (Rogerus le Barber) was admitted in 1290 – eighteen years before the first recorded Barber of the London Company. The Exchequer accounts of York for 1346 tells us 'Payments to William de Bolton and Hugo de Kilvington, Barber-Surgeons, going from York to the Castle of Bamburgh to heal the said David de Brus who lay there, having been wounded with an arrow at the said battle [Neville's Cross, 1346], and to extract the arrow and to heal him with despatch ... £6.' David de Brus was the younger brother of Robert the Bruce, King of Scotland, and victor at Bannockburn. De Brus later became King David of Scotland. At any one time the Gild comprised twenty or so registered 'Barber-Surgeons' who cut hair, extracted teeth and performed all manner of surgical procedures. It took a seven year apprenticeship in order to become a full member; apprentices were trained in the 'humours' in the body and the phases of the moon. The best time for blood-letting, for example, depended as much on the signs of the zodiac as anything else.

## The Bar Convent

The Bar Convent is the oldest lived-in convent in England. It was established as a school for Catholic girls in 1686 by Frances Bedingfield, an early member of Mary Ward's

'Ladies at the Bar' in 1900.

Institute, in response to Sir Thomas Gascoigne's demand: 'We must have a school for our daughters'. Sir Thomas, a local Catholic landowner, provided £450 to set up a boarding school; this was followed in 1699 by a free day school. Frances Bedingfield had been imprisoned in Ousebridge Gaol for her religious beliefs. For Catholics the seventeenth century was often a time of persecution and the Bar Convent was very much a clandestine community. Known as the 'Ladies at the Bar' the sisters wore plain grey day dresses rather than habits to avoid raising suspicion. The community suffered great poverty, persecution and imprisonment – not just for their faith but also for teaching that faith. However, it survived, and in 1727 was joined by Elizabeth Stansfield and Ann Aspinal who paid off the community's debts and in the 1760s demolished the original house to replace it with the fine Georgian house and integral chapel on the site today. April 1769 saw the first Mass to be held in the beautiful new Chapel, with its magnificent, but externally unobtrusive, neo-classical dome concealed beneath a pitched slate roof. Apart from the discreet dome, the building has many other integral features which betray the secret nature of its activities. The chapel is situated in the centre of the building so that it cannot be seen from the street; its plain windows reveal nothing of its ecclesiastical nature and there are no fewer than eight exits, providing escape routes for the congregation in the event of a raid. There is also a priest's hole which can still be seen today. The nuns who still live there belong to the Congregation of Jesus which was founded by Mary Ward (1585-1645).

Barker Tower, originally published in J. S. Fletcher's *Historic York*.

## Barker Tower

Next to North Street Postern, the tower dates from the early fourteenth century; it was given a new roof in the seventeenth century and was restored in 1840, 1930 and in 1970. The name derives from the barkers who stripped bark off oak trees to be used by tanners; hence nearby Tanner's Moat and Tanner Row. A chain was slung across the **Ouse** here as a line of defence and to prevent merchants from entering the city without paying tolls. Uses over the years include a boom tower and a mortuary from 1879.

## Barley Hall

Parts of Barley Hall go back as far as 1360, when the Hall was built as the York town house for Nostell Priory , the Augustinian monastery near Wakefield, by Thomas de Dereford, the Prior from 1337 to 1372. The Priors of Nostell were prebendary canons of **York Minster** and attended ceremonies, services and business meetings in the city; a hostel, therefore, made good commercial sense. However, by the fifteenth century, the Priory had fallen on hard times and Barley Hall was leased out to private tenants. A new wing was added in about 1430 and in 1460 it was rented out to William Snawsell – goldsmith, Master of the **Royal Mint** in York, MP for York, Alderman and **Lord Mayor of York** in 1468. By the seventeenth century it was subdivided into a number of smaller dwellings so that the 'screens passage' – the internal corridor area at the end of the Great Hall – came to be used as a public short-cut through from **Stonegate** to Swinegate. To this day it remains a public right-of-way, known as Coffee Yard.

By Victorian times, the house was 'a warren of tradesmen's workshops' and its last use before being sold for redevelopment in 1984 was as a plumber's workshop and showroom. The Hall was painstakingly restored to its former glory and it re-opened to the public in 1993. Barley Hall is named after Professor Maurice Barley, founder president of York Archaeological Trust.

## Bedern

An unsavoury, violent and impoverished place at the best of times with 300 people sharing just five toilets according to one report. On 10 October 1868 *The Yorkshire Gazette* reported on what was probably a typical day in Bedern with this encounter between John Rohan, Patrick Muldowney, Michael McMennamy and Bridget Rohan: 'Complainant [McMennamy] went out of his own house ... when John Rohan went behind him and struck him on the head with a poker ... two girls were fighting at the same time ... and notwithstanding the blow he tried to separate them and then Muldowney struck him with half a brick ... and while prostrate Bridget went out with a rolling pin and gave him some rattlers on the head, and the others kicked him ... John Rohan and Molly Rohan were also charged with assaulting Thomas McMennamy, son of the above-named complainant ... the girl struck him with an iron bolt and also bit his finger'.

Bedern Chapel.

## Bedern Hall

The first home of the thirty-six Vicars Choral of **York Minster** from 1349, the covered way was allowed by Richard II and made it easy for the vicars to get to the Minster, and to avoid the 'common people'. The present Hall dates from 1370 and was used until 1650 after which time in the nineteenth century it became a 'sad spectacle of poverty and wretchedness' when divided into slum tenements, largely for Irish navvies. The Gilds of **Freemen**, Master Builders and the Company of Cordwainers now occupy the Hall, restored in 1984. Cordwainers worked in 'cordwan', a type of shoe leather named after the Spanish town of Cordoba, the principal mediaeval source of this leather. The 1272 Freemens Rolls list over 200 Cordwainers here: the first entry is 'Thomas de Fulford, Cordwainer'. At the end of the sixteenth century the gild's senior officials, known as Searchers, were empowered to inspect all leather and shoes coming into York, rejecting any they found to be of inferior quality.

## Bettys

The neo-Georgian building in **St Helen's Square** was fitted out by Ward and Leckenby in 1937. The story of Bettys begins in September 1907 when a twenty-two-year-old Fritz Butzer arrived in England from Switzerland with no English and less of any idea of how to reach a town that sounded vaguely like 'Bratwurst', where a job awaited him. Fritz eventually landed up in Bradford and found work with a Swiss confectioners called Bonnet & Sons at 44 Darley Street. Cashing in on the vogue for all things French, Fritz changed his name to Frederick Belmont; he opened his first business in July 1919 – a cafe in Cambridge Crescent, Harrogate, on three floors fitted out to the highest standards. In 1936 Frederick travelled on the maiden voyage of *The Queen Mary*. He was so impressed that he commissioned the ship's designers to turn what had been an old furniture shop in York into his most sophisticated tea rooms – and that is what you still get in the art deco upstairs function room. J. E. Mcdonald was the first of many airmen to scratch their names on the mirror here in what became known as the **Briefing Room** during the Second World War, in February 1945.

## Bile Beans

One of York's famous surviving ghost adverts on Lord Mayor's Walk. Apart from ensuring good health, bright eyes and keeping you slim a nightly dose of the laxative beans was always good for 'inner health'. Other ghost adverts survive on **Stubbs'** old building on Merchantgate and on the Heslington Road promoting John Smith's Magnet Ales.

## Bishopthorpe

The original name was Thorpe as given in *Doomsday*, then Thorpe-on-Ouse in 1194; in 1275 we find Biscupthorpe. In 1202 the monks of St Andrews at Fishergate built the first church here and the name changed to Andrewthorpe, Thorpe St Andrew or St Andrewthorpe; this changed to Bishopthorpe in the thirteenth century when Archbishop Walter de Grey bought the manor house and presented it to the Dean and Chapter of **York Minster**. Bishopthorpe Palace was thus born; it has been the residence

The Gateway in 1907. The card was sent from the Station Hotel in York and reads, 'You will wonder me been [*sic*] here we have come to the races with the boss.'

of the **Archbishop of York** ever since and is currently the home of Dr John Sentamu. In 1323 a truce was signed here between Edward II and Robert the Bruce after the Battle of Bannockburn. Archbishop Drummond's renovation of the Palace in 1763 produced the Strawberry Gothick west front and gatehouse. The 1832 Reform Bill saw rioters try to overrun the Palace, incensed by Archbishop Harcourt's lack of support.

### Bitch Daughter Tower
On **Baile Hill** it has in its time been pressed into service as the King's prison until 1868, a Civil War guardhouse and as a cow shed. It was originally three storeys high but the upper rooms were quarried to repair **Ouse Bridge** in 1567. Early names include 'Biche Doughter' in 1566 and 'le bydoutre' in 1451.

### Blackburne, Lancelot – Archbishop and Pirate
Blackburne died in 1743; he was **Archbishop of York** from 1724 until his death before which he did time as a paid spy of Charles II in 1681, and as a pirate in the Caribbean in the 1680s. He reputedly drank ale and smoked a pipe during confirmations, behaviour typical of the man and described as follows: 'His behaviour was seldom of a standard to be expected of an archbishop ... in many respects it was seldom of a standard to be expected of a pirate'.

## The Black Swan, Coney Street

One of York's crucial coaching houses; this one was the staging post for the London to York four day journey, starting at *The Black Swan*, Holborn.

# YORK Four Days Stage-Coach.

Begins on Friday the 12th of April 1706

ALL that are defirous to pafs from *London* to *York*, or from *York* to *London* or any other Place on that Road: Let them Repair to the *Black Swan* in *Holbourn* in *London* and to the *Black Swan* in *Coney-ftreet* in *York*

At both which Places they may be received in a Stage Coach every *Monday, Wednefday* and *Friday*, which performs the whole Journey in Four Days. (if God permits.) And fets forth at Five in the Morning.

And returns from *York* to *Stamford* in two days, and from *Stamford* by *Huntington* to *London* in two days more. And the like Stages on their return.

Allowing each Paffenger 14l. in eight, and all above 3d a Pound

Performed By { Benjamin Kingman Henry Harrifon. Walter Baynes,

Alfo this gives Notice that *Newcaftle* Stage Coach, fets out from York, every Monday, and Friday, and from Newcaftle every Monday, and Friday.

*Rec.d. in pt. 05-00. of Mr. Bodingfild for Monday the 3 of June 1706 p.s.*

## YORK COACHING DAYS.

FAC-SIMILE OF THE COACHING NOTICE IN 1706.

The c_____            the George Inn Coach
Office, are as follow :—

To London, the Wellington, at a quarter past four in the afternoon, and arrives in
    London next afternoon at half past three o'clock.
To Newcastle and Edinbro', the Wellington, at a quarter past two in the afternoon,
    and arrives at Newcastle the same night, and Edinbro' next night at eight o'clock.
To Selby and Leeds, at half past three o'clock in the afternoon.
To Scarbro' and Sheffield, (during the season), at two o'clock in the afternoon.

The "*Old Judges' Lodgings,*" mentioned at page 106, were
formerly opposite to this Inn.

## THE BLACK SWAN INN, AND
## COACH OFFICE,

Are a little beyond the Old Judges' Lodgings, the former being
kept by Mr. Judd, and allowed to be by far the largest and the
best Inn in the city.

The COACH OFFICE is, and has long been, under the direction
of Mr. Dobson, who has favoured the writer with the following
official report of the times of arrival and departure of the different
mails and post coaches which come to and go from that office :—

### ARRIVALS.

| | H. | M. | | | H. | M. | |
|---|---|---|---|---|---|---|---|
| Leeds Wellington | 10 | 0 | night. | Whitby Neptune | 12 | 30 | noon. |
| London Mail | 5 | 0 | evening. | Hull Trafalgar | 1 | 0 | afternoon. |
| Scarbro' Mail | 8 | 0 | evening. | Newcastle Wellington | 3 | 45 | afternoon. |
| Hull Mail | 8 | 0 | evening. | Leeds Blue | 12 | 0 | noon. |
| Manchester Mail | 5 | 0 | evening. | London Wellington | 1 | 30 | afternoon. |
| Carlisle Express | 7 | 0 | morning. | Edinbro' Mail | 6 | 30 | morning. |
| Newcastle Express | 10 | 0 | night. | Hull Mail | 3 | 30 | afternoon. |
| London Express | 7 | 30 | morning. | Manchester Mail | 5 | 0 | morning. |
| Leeds Highflyer | 6 | 0 | evening. | Scarbro' Blue | 12 | 0 | noon. |
| Sheffield Transit | 1 | 30 | afternoon. | Harrogate Tally-Ho | 10 | 0 | morning. |

### DEPARTURES.

| | H. | M. | |
|---|---|---|---|
| Leeds, Manchester, Nottingham, and Kendal Wellington (Sundays excepted) | 6 | 0 | morning. |
| London Mail | 7 | 0 | morning. |
| Scarbro' Mail | 7 | 0 | morning. |
| Hull Mail | 7 | 0 | morning. |
| Leeds and Manchester Mail | 7 | 0 | morning. |
| Carlisle and Glasgow Express, every Monday, Wednesday, and Friday | 8 | 0 | morning. |
| Newcastle and Edinbro' Express (Sundays excepted) | 8 | 0 | morning. |
| London Express (Saturdays excepted) | 11 | 0 | morning. |
| Leeds and Manchester Highflyer, by Wetherby (Sundays excepted) | 9 | 0 | morning. |
| Sheffield and Birmingham Transit (Sundays excepted) | 2 | 0 | afternoon. |
| Whitby Neptune (Sundays excepted) | 2 | 0 | afternoon. |
| Hull Trafalgar (Sundays excepted) | 2 | 0 | afternoon. |
| Newcastle and Edinbro' Wellington | 2 | 0 | afternoon. |
| Leeds Blue (Sundays excepted) | 2 | 0 | afternoon. |
| London Wellington | 4 | 0 | afternoon. |
| Newcastle and Edinbro' Mail | 5 | 0 | evening. |
| Hull Mail | 7 | 30 | evening. |
| Manchester Mail | 9 | 0 | evening. |

SUMMER COACHES.

| | H. | M. | |
|---|---|---|---|
| Scarbro' Old True Blue (Sundays excepted) | 1 | 0 | noon. |
| Harrogate Tally Ho (Sundays excepted) | 2 | 0 | afternoon. |

## The Black Swan, Peasholme Green

*The Black Swan* in Peasholme Green; former coaching station, haunted and also known as *The Mucky Duck* it is one of the oldest licensed houses in York. Originally though it was the home of William Bowes, former Sheriff, **Mayor** and MP between 1417 and 1428. It still has a fine oak staircase and a magnificent Delft fireplace. The upstairs room was used for illegal cock-fights; the grill used by the guard to watch the stairs can still be seen. General Wolfe lived here in 1726; it was the HQ of the York Layerthorpe Cycling Club from 1834. The Leeds Arms (closed 1935) was next door on the corner of Haymarket; the Woolpack was over the road.

## Bleasdale, Pharmaceutical Manufacturers

1780 saw the establishment of John Dale's Bleasdale Ltd, manufacturing and wholesale chemists behind Colliergate. A visitor to the firm in the 1930s leaves us with the following description: 'after traversing a dark corridor, found ourselves confronted by a locked door – the entrance to the Poison Rooms . For the first time in my life I saw samples of raw opium – and very disinteresting they looked.' He would also have seen barrels of black beer, cod liver oil and machinery for grinding liquorice, trimming rhubarb and grinding poppies. Other pharmaceutical and chemical manufacturers included Wright and Prest in Pavement, Edward Wallis and Son in **Bedern** and Thomas Bishop at North Street Postern. There was also Raimes and Company from 1818 in **Micklegate** and Henry Richardson and Company, fertilizer makers founded in 1824 at Skeldergate Postern in Clementhorpe.

## Blind Tom, The Inexplicable Phenomenon

**York Theatre Royal** was the venue in 1853 for a concert by Miss Greenfield, a black former slave girl; reviews in the *Yorkshire Gazette* were very favourable. In 1866 we heard that 'Blind Tom is Coming! Blind Tom, the Inexplicable Phenomenon' who had recently wowed audiences at the St James's and Egyptian Halls in London (**York Herald**, 20 October). He too was an ex-slave and a protégé of **Charles Dickens** who counted him as a 'valued friend'. Tom was a 'make weight' thrown into the deal when his mother was bought by a tobacco-planter: 'a lump of black flesh born blind, and with the vacant grin of idiocy'. Notwithstanding, he turned out to be a gifted pianist and a success on the novelty and trick circuit: for example, 'his most confusing feat was to play one air with his left hand, another with his right in a different key, whilst he sang a third tune in a different key again ... experts such as the Head of Music at Edinburgh testified to his accuracy'.

## The Blue Bell

York's smallest pub is in Fossgate. It was built in 1798 when the back of the pub faced on to Fossgate and the front was in **Lady Peckett's Yard**. The **Rowntrees** were responsible for turning it around in 1903, no doubt because one of their Adult schools was in Lady Peckett's Yard. York City FC held their board meetings here; in the Second World War it served as a soup kitchen. Women were barred from the public bar until the 1990s.

## The Bluecoat School

Founded in 1705 as a charity school for forty poor boys by York Corporation in **St Anthony's Hall**. The blue coats worn by the boys were modelled on the uniform of Christ's Hospital School, originally in Greyfriars, London. A Greycoat School for twenty poor girls was founded at the same time in Marygate where the girls were trained for a life in domestic service with classes which included wool spinning.

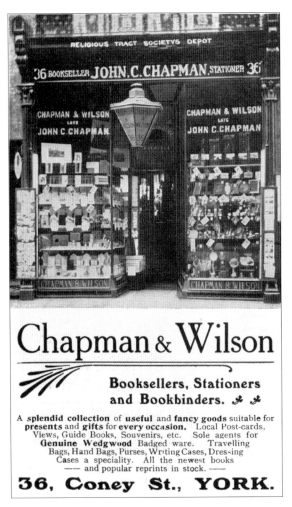

Advertisement for Chapman & Wilson booksellers.

Minerva, goddess of learning and wisdom, at the top of Stonegate.

## Bookselling in York

Arthur Andersons (Southeran's), Booksellers was in Coney Street in 1837, the latest in a long line of York booksellers stretching back to Francis Hildyard's shop established 'at the sign of The Bible, Stonegate' in 1682. In 1763 this became John Todd and Henry Sotheran until 1774 when Sotheran set up on his own next to St Helen's church soon moving across the Square to where the Savings Bank was. Henry Cave's late-eighteenth-century Todd's Book and Print Warehouse, as with many booksellers of the time, was something of an apothecary too with a popular line in rat poison, negus and lemonade and similar preparations and confections. Roman busts watched over the 30,000 or so books. **William Alexander** was another bookseller, in **Castlegate**; Ann Alexander was the author of a pamphlet campaigning against the exploitation of children and specifically against the employment of climbing boys in 1817. The Book Saloon at 6 Micklegate stocked 'the largest and best selection in the North of England', according to *York in 1837*, which goes on to tell us that the bookshop 'meets the demand for healthy literature engendered by the rapid growth of education and educational facilities'. Thomas Wilson at the Dryden's Head – Bookseller, Stationer, Printer Etc sold fancy goods, local guidebooks and postcards in **Coney Street**, before that in High Ousegate and **Pavement**, and Cash Stationery Store in Bridge Street offered 'a wide range of funeral cards'; John Wolstenholme sold books in Minster Gates, his building graced by his brother's fine statue of Minerva. Other evidence for this bookish aspect of York society are the red **Printer's Devil** and Coffee Yard off Stonegate. See also **Thomas C. Godfrey, Bookseller.** Today, independent bookselling survives with the Little Apple near the Minster and the Barbican Bookshop in Fossgate.

Bootham Bar in 1906. This card was sent from 'your loving pupil Alice Russell' to her teacher, Miss Batley at Seacroft School in Leeds. Alice tells her, 'Dear teacher, I have enjoyed my holidays very much.'

## Bootham

This elegant street was originally called Galmanlith and extended from **Bootham Bar** to Marygate. No. 49 was lived in by **Joseph Rowntree**; called Lady Armstrong's Mansion it cost £4,500 and included 6 acres of land; it was later taken over by **Bootham School**. **W. H. Auden's** house was opposite.

## Bootham Bar

Bootham Bar (originally Buthum which means at the booths and signifies the markets which used to be held here) stands on the north-western gateway of the Roman fortress. A door knocker was added to the Bar in 1501 for the use of Scotsmen (and others presumably) seeking admission to the city. The barbican came down in 1831 and the wall steps went up in 1889; a statue of Ebrauk, the pre-Roman founder of York, once stood nearby. Thomas Mowbray's severed head was stuck here in 1405 and the Earl of Manchester bombarded the Bar in 1644 during the Civil war. The removal of the barbican was due in part to complaints by residents of Clifton: 'not fit for any female of respectability to pass through' on account of the droppings of animals en route to the cattle market and its use as a urinal by pedestrians. The three statues on the top were carved in 1894 and feature a mediaeval **mayor**, a mason and a knight; the mason is holding a model of the restored Bar.

Bootham Bar showing the taxi stand with horse and carriage in attendance.

## Bootham School

**William Tuke** (1732-1822) first raised the idea in 1818 of setting up a boys' school in York for the sons of Quakers 'and any children of the opulent who will submit themselves to the general system of diet and discipline'. In 1822 premises on Lawrence Street were leased from the **Retreat**, and the school opened in early 1823 as the York Friends Boys' School, or 'The Appendage'. In 1829 it had become known as Yorkshire Quarterly Meeting Boys' School – its official name until 1889 – even after it had moved to 20 (now 51) **Bootham** in 1846. It was the school's proximity to the River Foss that triggered the move to more salubrious premises; one master even carried a pistol to shoot the rats; cholera was also a problem. In the late nineteenth century many of the Rowntree family boys were educated at Bootham; one of them, **Arthur Rowntree** (or Chocolate Jumbo to give him his nickname), was Headmaster (1899-1927). The school had a tradition of taking disadvantaged boys from the Lawrence Street area on a Lads' Camp, usually at Robin Hood's Bay, and this endured well into the twentieth century. Arthur Rowntree said: 'We are proud to be in the tradition of promoting friendship between all classes'. A number of staff and scholars were influential in the political and social reforms of their times, not least **Seebohm Rowntree** (Bootham 1882-87).

## Bootham Natural History Society

Started in 1834 by John Ford, superintendent or head from 1829 to 1865. Its full name was 'The Natural History, Literary and Polytechnic Society' and as such was the umbrella organisation for many other clubs. The school was moved to Roman Catholic Ampleforth during the Second World War; Donald Gray, the head at the time, is reputed to have addressed the combined school as 'Friends, Romans and Countrymen'. Bootham was not the only boys' Quaker School in York: in 1827 the Hope Street British School was established and attended by many children of Friends; it was slightly unusual because, in addition to the usual curriculum, it taught the working of the Electric Telegraph with the Electric Telegraph Company supplying the instruments and the school reciprocating by supplying the company with clerks.

## Bootham Snails
In 1899 almost the entire school was destroyed by fire: a keen pupil was boiling snail shells in the Natural History room when he was summoned by the bell for reading, and the snails were left boiling all night ... on being informed by the fire brigade that his school was a smouldering shell the headmaster fell on his sword and promptly resigned. The accidental arsonist later became a farmer and blew himself up while uprooting a tree.

## Botterill's Repository for Horses
Built in 1884 next to **Lendal Bridge** it was reduced in height by a half in 1965 when it became a car dealers. Patrick Nuttgens described the original building as 'an exotic red and yellow Byzantine building with ramps inside, up which the horses were led to their stalls – a kind of multi-story horse car park'. It was frequently used by patrons of the 1868 Yorkshire Club for gentlemen (River House) in from the country, just over Lendal Bridge.

## Boyes
The devastating fire at the Boyes building on Ouse Bridge, 8 November 1910 started on the second of six floors when paper decorations in the toy department were set alight by a nearby gas lamp. Despite the best efforts of the fire brigade, assisted by the **Rowntree** Fire Brigade, the building was a smouldering shell six hours later. Boyes' Scarborough store also burnt down, in 1914. The old shop had been trading since 1906; Boyes' new shop was completed in July 1912 and closed down in 1983, to reopen in Goodramgate in 1987.

## Bridgend School and Brigadier Gerard
A private residence and the Gas Works Social Club were other uses for this school building which was extended and converted into *The Brigadier Gerard* in Monkgate in 1984. The name comes from the famous racehorse which won seventeen of its eighteen races – the single defeat was at York in 1972. The horse in turn was named after Brigadier Etienne Gerard, the hero in Arthur Conan Doyle's *Exploits of Brigadier Gerard*, a series of short stories originally published in *The Strand* magazine between 1894 and 1903.

## The Briefing Room
On 1 February 1945 J. E. Mcdonald was the first of 600 airmen to scratch their names on the mirror at **Bettys** during the Second World War. Also known as Betty's Bar or the Dive it was a regular haunt of the hundreds of airmen stationed in and around York; these included many Canadians from Number 6 Bomber Group. One signatory, Jim Rogers, borrowed a waitress' diamond ring to scratch his name on the mirror.

The poster advertising the Meeting of the British Association at York, August 1881.

### The British Association for the Advancement of Science

The British Association for the Advancement of Science (now known as The British Science Association) was founded with the help of the **Yorkshire Philosophical Society** and held its inaugural meeting at the **Yorkshire Museum** in 1831. The astronomical **Observatory** was built in the **Museum Gardens** soon after. It is the oldest working observatory in Yorkshire.

### Burton, Dr John

One time resident in the **Red House** and the model for **Laurence Sterne's** Dr Slop in *The Life and Times of Tristram Shandy*, as depicted in Hogarth's frontispiece for the first edition. Burton, a medical doctor educated at Cambridge, Leiden and Rheims, also authored the unfinished *Monasticon Eboracense*, an ecclesiastical history of Yorkshire in 1758; he was incarcerated in York Castle after his involvement in the 1745 Jacobite Rebellion as 'a suspicious person to His Majesty's government'.

### Burton Stone

At the junction of Burton Stone Lane and **Bootham**. The stone with its three holes is something of a mystery. It may have been a rallying point for soldiers before going off to war or it may be a plague stone. Its holes would either have held a cross or have been filled with vinegar and coins deposited: the money allowed those quarantined beyond to buy food; the vinegar acted as a disinfectant.

## Butter Market

The site of York's butter market and the butter stand was in Micklegate. York was, in the mid-eigtheenth century, the country's largest depot for the collection of butter for shipment by sea to the London market. The stand was originally in the yard of St Martin-cum-Gregory until 1764 when it was moved to the street, then demolished in 1828. The daily market was established in 1662 and formalised by Act of Parliament in 1722.

## Carr, John

Born 1723 Carr was **Lord Mayor** of York in 1770 and 1785; he lived on his estate at Askham Richard for most of his adult life. He designed the Crescent at Buxton; racecourse grandstands at York, Doncaster and Nottingham, prisons at Wakefield and Northallerton, Greta Bridge, Constable Burton Hall and Harewood House. His crowning achievement though is the magnificent **Fairfax House** in **Castlegate**, York.

## The Castle

Established as one of two castles by William I; Henry III rebuilt it in 1260 as part of the city defences which included the stone **Bar Walls** replacing wooden pallisades. More recently the site has housed a prison and, today, the **Castle Museum**. **Clifford's Tower** survives. The buildings here make up the 'Eye of the Ridings'.

The mighty castle walls encompassing the prison.

## Castlegate
The setting for Walter Scott's *The Severn Stars* where Jeanie Deans stayed en route to London in *Heart of Midlothian*.

## The Castle Museum
York Castle Museum opened in 1938 and is one of Britain's leading museums of everyday life. It is famous for its Victorian street, Kirkgate, named after the museum's founder, Dr John Lamplugh Kirk, a Pickering doctor who collected everyday objects, his 'bygones', and for whom the Museum was converted from the Women's **Prison** as somewhere to keep them safe for future generations.

## The Cattle Market
A cattle market existed here from the fifteenth century. The opening in 1855 of the 6-acre cattle market in Paragon Street led to the reopening of Fishergate Bar to enable cattle to be driven through; it also saw the end of the time-honoured practice of keeping livestock behind butchers' shops and slaughtered on site, as happened in **Shambles** for many years. The market building comprised forty-four pens which could hold 616 fat cattle, some less fat ones and 6,750 sheep. It served the city for nearly 150 years when it moved to Murton after closing in 1971; it was demolished in 1976. The Barbican Centre, refurbished in 2011, was built on part of the cattle market site in the late 1970s.

The old castle market.

## Centenary Chapel

Or Central Methodist Chapel, in Colliergate. This grandiose building dates from 1840 and gets its name from the fact that it was built as a cathedral to Methodism and celebrates 100 years of Methodism. The central hall seats 1500 people.

## The Chapter House

This octagonal building at the **Minster** was completed in 1286 and was the meeting place for the Dean and Chapter. It was designed to emphasize the equality implicit in these two offices: this explains the seats around the edge – not in the middle – and the poor acoustics which meant that anyone speaking from the centre could barely be heard on the perimeter. The rich variety of carvings are said to represent characters from the masons' own lives.

## Chocolate Festival – York 800

Part of the York 800 celebrations this mark's York's status as the chocolate capital of Britain with a series of events marking the contribution **Rowntree**, **Terry** and **Craven** have made to the city's economy and its social fabric.

## Cholera

The first British case of the 1826 Bengal pandemic was in Sunderland in September 1831 reaching York in June 1832 at Hagworm's Nest off Skeldergate. The disease led to 450 cases and claimed 185 people who were buried in a new cemetery opposite the **railway station**. Twenty headstones remain despite efforts in 1925 to secularise the area to improve access to the station. 32,000 people died throughout the country.

## Cinemas

In 1919 York had no shortage of picture houses; popularity continued to grow and in the 1940s they included *The Picture House*, **Coney Street** opened in 1915; the *Tower* in New Street (so small it only had four rows in the balcony); *St George's* in 1921 (next to **Fairfax House**); the *Electric* opened in 1911, renamed the *Scala* in 1951; the *Regent* (Acomb); the *Grand* (Clarence St from 1919); the 1937 art deco **Odeon** in Blossom Street and the art deco *Clifton*; the *Rialto* in Fishergate – formerly the *Casino* and the *City Picture Palace* in 1914; it promoted itself as offering 'World Famous artists of Radio, Stage, Screen and Concert Platform; World Famous Orchestras' as well as 'World famous Films'. The *Clifton* (cinema and ballroom) was the first in York to have an organ that rose up in front of the screen; its first film was *Sabu the Elephant Boy*. The first cinema, though, was the converted Wesleyan Chapel known as the *New Street Palace of Varieties* which opened in 1909 with a film showing the Messina earthquake and tsunami of 1908.

## City Art Gallery

A temporary building was erected in the grounds of Bootham Park Hospital for the first *Yorkshire Fine Art and Industrial Exhibition*. Made entirely from wood and glass the front was decorated with Royal coats of arms and those of the patrons. The

City Art Gallery – the temporary 1866 building.

Italianate building which houses the gallery opened its doors to the public in 1879 for the second *Exhibition,* inspired by the Great Exhibition in London of 1851. The York exhibition attracted more than half a million visitors and made a profit of £12,000. In 1892 it became the **City Art Gallery**. Prominent in Exhibition Square is the 1911 statue of **William Etty.** The building continued in use from 1880 as the Yorkshire Fine Art and Industrial Institution until 1892 when it was purchased by the City Council. The original building had a 'Great Exhibition Hall' at the rear with room for 2,000 people. This was a venue for boxing and cock fighting as well as exhibitions; it was damaged by bombs during the Second World War and demolished in 1942. The Gallery's collection was initiated in 1882 when a retired horse dealer from Poppleton, John Burn, was persuaded to leave his collection of paintings to the city rather than to his first choice, the National Gallery. Apart from numerous paintings of York and its buildings there are many works by **William Etty.** Every year between 1950 and 1962 an artist was paid £50 to produce a picture of York: L. S. Lowry's painting of **Clifford's Tower** is one of the results. The gallery is currently undergoing a major two-year refurbishment.

## The City Walls

The walls were built in the thirteenth and fourteenth century on a rampart dating from the ninth and eleventh centuries. They survive for the best part of their 2 miles plus length as do the four Bars and thirty-seven internal towers. Four of the six posterns and nine other towers are lost or have been rebuilt. The walls for the most part are 6 feet wide and 13 feet high. They were breached in two places in the 1840s to allow access to York's second **railway station** and to a goods depot known as the Sack Warehouse.

A fine 1960s view of York from the walls.

## City of York

York was granted a Royal Charter by King John in 1212, permitting the city to take charge of its financial affairs and to trade freely. The people of York created a council led by a **Lord Mayor**. 800 years later the city celebrated that momentous occasion with the year long series of events and festivities that was **York 800**.

## Clifford Street

Developed in 1881. The Rechabite Buildings opened in 1883 followed by the York Institute of Popular Science, Art and Literature and the new Friends' Meeting House in 1884 and the Law Courts and Police Station in 1892.

## Clifford's Tower

Originally King's Tower, or even the 'Minced Pie', but from 1596 named after Francis Clifford, Earl of Cumberland, who restored it for use as a garrison after it had been partly dismantled by Robert Redhead in 1592. An alternative etymology comes from Roger de Clifford whose body was hung there in chains in 1322. Built in wood by William the Conqueror when he visited to establish his northern HQ in 1190, it was burnt down when 150 terrified York **Jews** sought sanctuary here from an anti-semitic mob; faced with the choice of being killed or forced baptism, many committed suicide; 150 others were slaughtered. It was rebuilt in stone by King John and Henry III as a quadrilobate between 1245 and 1259 as a self-contained stronghold and royal residence; it housed the kingdom's Treasury in the fourteenth century. Robert Aske, one of the prime movers in the Pilgrimage of Grace, was hanged here on 12 July 1537. On

*Above:* Clifford's Tower and the 1777 assize courts on the left in the 1920s before the walls and the Governor's House (on the right) were demolished in 1935. Note the deer. From an 1841 lithograph by F. Beford published by John Glaisby, bookseller of Coney Street.

*Right:* A picnic on the motte around the tower in the days when it was in private hands and the owners planted trees and other vegetation. From an engraving by John Charles Varrall after W. H. Bartlett in 1828.

23 April 1684 the roof was blown off during an over-enthusiastic seven-gun salute. In 1699 Lady Suzanna Thomson sold it to Richard Sowray who wanted it as an attractive backdrop to his nearby house; the *York Spy* or the *Northern Atalantis*, reported that 'an old Crabbed humorist defaced the Mount to enlarge his gardens'. Deer grazed around the tower for many years; it became part of the **prison** in 1825. The motte is 48 feet high and the tower itself 33 feet. The moat was fed by a diversion from the Ouse.

### Clitherow, Margaret

Margaret Clitherow's oratory is in **Shambles**. Margaret was the wife of John Clitherow, a butcher who lived here at number 35 (or possibly at number 10). During Elizabeth I's persecution of Catholics, Margaret was first jailed in 1577 for not attending church. She was jailed twice more at York **Castle**, the second time for twenty months. Between 1582 and 1583 five priests were executed at **Tyburn** on **Knavesmire** and, when not in jail, Margaret would go at night to the gallows to visit the bodies. She was found guilty in 1586 of 'harbouring and maintaining Jesuits and priests, enemies to Her Majesty'. The usual penalty was hanging, but, due to her refusal to offer a plea at her trial at the City assizes in the **Guildhall** (called Common Hall at the time), she was sentenced to be pressed to death by Sir John Clenche (*peine forte et dure*) by having a door weighted with nearly half a ton of boulders placed on top of her at the tollbooth on **Ouse Bridge**. Within fifteen minutes she was dead. Elizabeth I wrote to the citizens of York in horror at the treatment meted out to a fellow woman. Margaret was beatified in 1929 and canonised in 1970 by Pope Paul VI who described her as the 'Pearl of York'. Her embalmed hand is in the **Bar Convent**. A church in Haxby is dedicated to her.

A 1912 York postcard sent from Paris showing the York City Coat of Arms.

## Coat of Arms

Earliest records of York's Coat of Arms comes in the Corporation minutes of 1 February 1587 which tell us that the **Lord Mayor** received the Coat of Arms of the City, on parchment, from the Queen's Herald of Arms. The common features are the red cross of St George, reflecting the city's ecclesiastical importance, and the five gold lions of England, underlying its Royalist leanings. The lions are 'passant' (walking) and 'guardant' (facing the viewer): they are, therefore active and alert. The civic sword and mace show the city's powers of self-government under the mayor; the sword was presented to the city by Richard II in 1387; he thus allowed it to be carried before the mayor on ceremonial occasions; a charter in 1396 allowed a similar right for the mace.

## Cocoa Works Magazine

**Rowntree's** house magazine. March 1902 saw the publication of the inaugural issue of the *Cocoa Works Magazine*, or *CWM* ; the last edition was in May 1986. For eight-four years it provided an intriguing and detailed record of life at Rowntree from the board to the shop floor. Subtitled *A Journal in the Interest of the Empoyees of Rowntree & Co Ltd, York*, its purpose was to keep everyone informed about what was going on at all levels.

## Coffee Houses

There was a plethora of coffee houses in York from 1669 – there are at least thirty recorded amongst which were *Parker's* in Minster Yard – next to a bowling alley as shown on Horsley's 1896 map; the *Garrick* in Low Petergate; *Wombwell and Wink's*, *Harrison's* in Petergate and later Nessgate; *Iveson's*, also in Petergate, *Duke's* near to the **Ouse Bridge**; and *Brigg's* on the corner of **Stonegate** and Coffee Yard – as well as **William Tuke's** roasting house. As one of thirty-one York tea dealers in 1823 and importers of tea, coffee and chocolate the Tuke's were the exclusive holders in the north of England of a licence which permitted the processing of coffee beans and the sale of roasted coffee, tea and chocolate. Chicory was grown around York for a time in the nineteenth century and sold to merchants who sold it on as an additive to coffee. One such merchant was Henry Wilberforce (d. 1876) of Walmgate, succeeded by his son William Wilkinson Wilberforce, **Mayor** in 1880.

## Cold War Bunker

Opened, or rather closed, in 1961 this piece of Cold War furniture was officially No 20 Group Royal Observer HQ operated by UKWMO, the UK Warning and Monitoring Organisation. Its role was to function as one of twenty-nine monitoring and listening posts in the event of a nuclear explosion. Decommissioned in 1991, English Heritage have opened it to the public to enable them to see the decontamination areas, living quarters, communications centre and operations rooms.

## Collins, Wilkie (1824-1889)

A frequent visitor; he set his 1862 novel, *No Name*, in the city describing a walk along the **walls** by Captain Wragge as 'one of the most striking scenes which England can show ... the majestic west front of York Minster soared over the city and caught the last brightest light of heaven on the summits of its lofty towers'.

Despite the decline of the combmaking industry and the departure of much of the gentry, York still retains some prestigious top-drawer services, as this 1930s advertisement shows: 'ici on parle Francais'!

## Comb Making & Hornbreaking

Comb making became a recognised craft in 1635 when the Livery Company of Combmakers received its charter. Demand increased as York's fashionability increased – to cater for the rapidly changing hairstyles amongst modish women, and men. Comb and horn breaking flourished around Hornpot Lane off Petergate (now Tonge's Court) – near to the slaughterhouses in **Shambles – Micklegate Bar** and Tanner Row. By 1784 there were sixty-five freemen, journeymen and apprentices engaged in the trade. Comb makers worked in ivory and tortoiseshell as well as in horn; books and manuscripts were covered with horn and the crockery of poor people was often made from horn. There is still a horn window in **Barley Hall**. One of the more successful comb companies was Joseph Rougier, a maker of drinking horns, combs and lanterns, from 1823 until 1931 – Rougier was descended from a Huguenot family of wigmakers and hairdressers and gave his name to the street near his Tanner Row works; another was George Steward & Son in Blossom Street. Rougier's son, Joseph (d.1842), was appointed Manufacturer of Ornamental Horn Shavings to Queen Victoria in 1837. The industry began to recede from 1796 when mechanisation was introduced.

## Commercial Academy

Established by a Mr Randall in the Thursday Market Hall, now **St Sampson's Square**, in 1748. The curriculum was nothing if not progressive and included: The Best English Authors; the Italian Method of Bookkeeping; the Terrestrial Globe Considered as a Map of the World with the Astronomical Parts of Geography.

The Hall of the Merchant Adventurers of the City of York, *c.* 1905.

## The Company of Merchant Adventurers of the City of York

A Merchant Adventurer was a merchant who risked his own money in pursuit of his trade or craft. For centuries, up until 1835 when the Municipal Corporations Act transferred control to local councils, the Guilds were all-powerful and controlled York's **trade and industry**. To do business in the city it was necessary to be elected a **Freeman** of the City: a man or a woman had to be a Freeman before membership was allowed to the craft guilds. The Merchant Adventurers Guild goes back to 1357 when a number of prominent York men and women joined together to form a religious fraternity and to build the **Merchant Adventurers' Hall**. By 1430 most members were merchants of one kind or another; they then set up a trading association or guild using the Great Hall to conduct their business affairs and to meet socially, to look after the poor in the **almshouses** in the Undercroft and to worship in the Chapel.

### The Company of Merchant Taylors in the City of York

One of seven guilds in York which date back to the thirteenth century and one of only three which have existed without break since mediaeval times. The Royal Charter of Incorporation of the Company was issued by King Charles II in 1662; however, the company can trace its origins back to the three mediaeval guilds of tailors, drapers and hosiers, the earliest references to which are the ordinances and register of members of 1387. The first reference to 'the land and hall of the fraternity of St John de Baptist' is in 1415 while the first mention of a York Taylors **almshouse** comes in 1446. The building in Aldwark, dates from 1446. In the early nineteenth century there were over forty drapers in York. There are two fine stained glass windows here by Henry Gyles, one dating from 1701.

### Coney Street

The earliest record of the name is in 1213 when it was called Cuningstreta, from the Viking word konungra for king and straet – street. Later writers refer to it as Cunny Street. So, it was, and is, King's street. Leak & Thorp's was built on the site of the fourteenth century Old George Inn, demolished in 1869. The fine clock outside **St Martin Le Grand** church dates from 1668; it was damaged in the **Baedeker Raid** ; restored in 1966 (complete with the **'Little Admiral'** with sextant who survived the raid) and in 2013 it is still telling us the time of day.

Coney Street with helpful policeman in the late 1950s.

## Constantine

Constantine the Great was the only Roman emperor to be proclaimed *Augustus* while in Britain, in AD 306; he converted to Christianity in a ceremony outside the Minster in 312 after seeing a vision of the cross when consulting his Roman gods before a battle. York, thereby, became an early, vital centre of Christianity. We have Constantine to thank for Christmas, for it was he who organised the first festivities celebrating Christ's birth. A marble head of Constantine was found during an excavation in **Stonegate.**

## Cooke, Thomas

Thomas Cooke came to York in 1829 and made his first telescope using the base of a whisky glass for a lens and a tin for the tube. In 1837 he opened his first instrument-making shop at 50 **Stonegate** with a loan of £100 from his wife's uncle. Cooke quickly gained a reputation for high quality and was soon making microscopes, opera glasses, spectacles, electrical machines, barometers, thermometers, globes, sundials and mathematical instruments as well as telescopes. By 1844 he had expanded and moved to 12 **Coney Street.**

Thomas Cooke on his revolutionary steamcar – second from the left.

## Cooke, Troughton & Simms – Optical Instrument Manufacturers

In 1856 Cooke moved into the Buckingham Works built on the site of the home of the second Duke of Buckingham at Bishophill – one of Britain's first purpose built telescope factories. He built a telescope for Prince Albert in 1860 and one for a Gateshead millionaire: the telescope tube was 32 feet long and the whole instrument weighed

nine tons: the biggest telescope in the world at the time. In 1893 H. D. Taylor, Optical Manager, designed the Cooke Photographic Lens which became the basic design for most camera lenses thereafter. In 1866 Thomas Cooke branched out into three-wheeled steam cars which reached the dizzy speed of 15 mph; they were, however, outlawed by the Road Act which prohibited vehicles which travelled in excess of 4 mph. In those days a man with a red flag had to walk in front of any vehicle not pulled by a horse. Cooke fitted his steam engine into a boat and travelled on the **Ouse**, free of horses and red flags. He died in 1868.

## County Hospital

York County Hospital opened in a rented house in 1740 in Monkgate. Before that, from 1614, the City Surgeon was responsible for medical care. In 1745 a purpose-built hospital opened on the same site with fifty beds: by 1750 2,417 patients had been treated. As a charitable hospital (where the financiers could choose who received treatment there) the County Hospital was not responsible for the city's sick poor; this led to the establishment of the **Dispensary**. The 1745 hospital building was demolished in 1851 and replaced with a new 100 bed hospital costing £11,000. In 1887 it merged with the York Eye Institution, opened in 1875. The present 600 bed York District Hospital opened in 1976 replacing the County Hospital, Fulford Hospital, Deighton Grove Hospital, Yearsley Bridge Hospital, Acomb Hospital, the Military Hospital and City Hospital. The eighteenth century also saw the founding of York **Lunatic Asylum** and the revolutionary **Retreat** for the care of the mentally ill.

*Opposite above:* A worker testing a theodolite in 1928.

*Opposite below:* Charles Piazzi Smyth's *Commencement of the Total Eclipse of July 28 1851 at Blue Island, Norway.* The telescopes pictured would have included some made by Cooke, Troughton & Simms.

*Right:* The Second World War war record of Rowntree & Co. Ltd.

## County Industries Ltd

In the Second World War many companies, Mars for example, were either closed for the duration, transformed into completely different companies in support of the war effort – **Rowntree's** 'became' County Industries Ltd – or else they hosted other war manufacturers: Rowntree, for example, manufactured *Oxford Marmalade* on behalf of Frank Cooper Ltd. The brief for County Industries Ltd was mainly to produce shell and mine fuses in the *Smarties* block.   In addition, 300 clerks of the Royal Army Pay Corps moved in as did York firm **Cooke, Troughton & Simms** for the manufacture of military optical instruments.   Out of the Cream Department came *National Milk Cocoa, Ryvita, Household Milk* and dried egg. The Card Box Mill swapped production of fancy boxes for supplies for the RASC, Northern Command.   Part of the Dining Block became a refuge for blitzed families, notably in the aftermath of the 1942 **Baedecker Raid**; a VAD hospital with 100 or so beds occupied the rest of the building. There was also a nursery to allow mothers of young children to come to work. At any one time sixty children were in occupation; cots were made by the work's joiners and the orchard became the playground.

## Coverdale, Miles

Born in York in 1488, as Bishop of Exeter he made the first translation of the *Bible* into English in 1539, printed and published it.

## Crafts and Trades in York

Butchers were focused in **Shambles**; other trades had similar concentrations. Ousegate and Castlegate were famous for their lorimers (makers of bits and bridles) and spurriers; cutlers were to be found near St Michael-le-Belfry; pinners at St Crux; girdlers at Girdlergate (Church Street), Tanners near North Street (hence Tanner's Moat and Tanner Row); fishmongers on the Foss and Ouse Bridges; parchment and leather workers and prostitutes at Harlot Hill (St Maurice's Road today), prostitutes also in Grope (Grape) Lane.

## Craven's

The company originated in 1803 when Joseph Hick set up as a twenty-nine year old in York as Kilner and Hick, confectioners. Kilner left town leaving Hick with the business which he relocated to 47 **Coney Street** next door to what was then the Leopard Inn, opposite **St Martin le Grand**. Mary Ann Hick was born in 1829 and in 1851 she married Thomas Craven who had served an apprenticeship with George Berry, later a partner at **Terry's**; he bought a building in Pavement from William Dove and a further site at 10 Coppergate, both of which expanded his own confectionery business. In 1860 Joseph Hick died and his estate was divided up between his three children. In 1862 Mary Ann's husband died leaving her with three young children to raise and two businesses to run. Near to starvation she took up the challenge, amalgamated the businesses, changed the name of the company to MA Craven, and ran it until her death in 1902. In 1881 her son, Joseph William, had joined the firm which became MA Craven & Son. There were four Craven's retail shops in the city, one of which, Craven's

Advertisement for Craven's.

Mary Ann Sweet Shop, was in the **Shambles** and featured a sweet museum on the first floor where visitors could see 150 years of the 'Art, Trade, Mystery and Business of the Confectioner'. Today the Craven brand is owned by Tangerine Confectionery which manufacturers sugar confectionery from their plant in Low Poppleton Lane.

### The Cries of York

York, like other cities, had its own repertoire of cries. Some of these were compiled in a penny book and published by J. Kendrew of Colliergate in 1811 'for the amusement of good children'. Typical are: 'Threepence a quart, Ripe Goosberries, Ripe gooseberries at York you'll buy, As cheap as cheap can be, Of many sorts you hear the cry, Pray purchase sir of me' and 'A list of horses that's to start On Knavesmire, and each name; With riders that are dressed so smart, Anxious the prize to claim'.

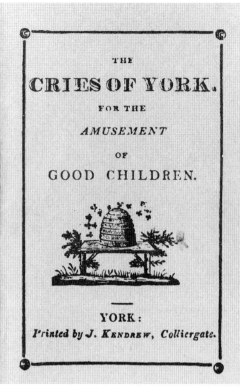

## Defoe, Daniel

'There is abundance of good company here, and abundance of good families live here, for the sake of the good company and cheap living; a man converses here with all the world as effectually as at London.' This is how Daniel Defoe generously described York in his , *A Tour Thro' The Whole Island Of Great Britain,* 1724. Much seems to have changed since the days of **William of Malmesbury** *qv.* Defoe's *Robinson Crusoe* opens with 'I was born in the year 1862, in the city of York, of a good family...'

## The De Grey Rooms

The De Grey Rooms is an elegant neo-classical building, paid for by public subscription in 1841-2 and designed by the architect George Townsend Andrews, renowned for his work on **York Railway Station**. The Rooms housed the officers' mess of the Yorkshire Hussars before the building went on to become a popular venue for balls, concerts and parties. They are named after Thomas Philip de Grey, who was the 2nd Earl de Grey and colonel-commandant of the Yorkshire Hussar Regiment. **Terry's Restaurant** managed the rooms in the 1930s. Since 2011 the Rooms have been annexed to the **Theatre Royal** next door, staging dance productions and thus taking it back to one of its early functions. Appropriately, York Theatre Royal hosted a ten hour Danceathon in April 2011 , to help raise the £50,000 needed for refurbishment.

## F. R. Delittle, Fine Art Printers

**Printers** at the Eboracum Letter Factory, 6 Railway Street (now George Hudson Street) later moving to Vine Street. Founded in 1888 they were publishers of the *Yorkshire Chronicle and Delittle's York Advertiser* which had a circulation of 12,000 copies in 1897. They also produced the *City Chronicle and Sheffield Advertiser;* staff numbered sixty in 1900. Books published included *Eboracum*, *The Yorkshire Road Book* and *Delittle's Picturesque York* as well as *York in 1837*. They were particularly noted for the world famous top quality wooden type used for railway posters, theatre bill boards and shop window advertisements. Delittle closed in 1997 but their fame lives on in the Type Museum in London which displays a reconstruction of the Delittle type room.

## Dickens, Charles

On one of his visits to York in 1838, Dickens describes in his *Letters* a visit to his friend, John Camidge, organist at the Minster, who showed him round. Dickens was particularly struck by 'the deep organ's bursting heart throb through the shivering air' and the Five Sisters Window. Dickens' story about the window appears in *Nicholas Nickleby* as the *Five Sisters of York*. Mr Micawber from *David Copperfield*, too, finds his origins in York, based as he is on a Richard Chicken, a feckless character who in 1847 worked in the same railway office as Albert Dickens, Charles' railway engineer brother. Chicken was also an actor and at one time a self-styled Professor of Elocution and Lecturer on Defective Annunciation.

Charles Dickens' York haunts, from an illustration by E. Ridsdale Tate published in T. P. Cooper's *With Dickens in Yorkshire.*

## The Dispensary

The York Dispensary, set up to look after York's sick poor (the **County Hospital** had no remit there), was originally in the **Merchant Adventurers' Hall**, moving to St Andrewgate and then, in 1828, to New Street. The next move was to the majestic, often overlooked, red brick building in **Duncombe Place** in 1851. Its noble mission, as recorded in *Baines' Directory* for 1823, was 'to dispense gratuitously advice, medicine and surgical assistance, to those who are unable to pay for them'. Medicines were free of charge and 600 or so children were vaccinated here 'without cost for the smallpox'. The corporation contributed £5 towards an apothecary's shop and one guinea a year for five years. After thirty or so years 42,488 patients had been seen with 28,851 cured.

## Domesday York

York's entry tells us about the 1,418 houses in 1086 with such detail as 'Odo the Crossbowman has three dwellings, of Forne and Orne ... Landric the carpenter has ten and half dwellings which the sheriff assigned to him'.

## Dorothy Wilson's School

Dorothy Wilson's **almshouse** and schoolroom stood on Foss Bridge. It is now converted to flats, but the building still bears the carved inscription recording the foundation in 1719 of Dorothy Wilson's Charity for the 'Maintenance of ten poor Women as also for the instruction in English, Reading, Writing and Clothing of twenty poor Boys for ever'. There is also a memorial tablet to Dorothy Wilson in St Denys Church.

## Drake, Francis

Drake (1696-1771) was an eminent York surgeon at **York County Hospital** and author of the landmark *Eboracum, or the History and Antiquities of the City of York*. Some things have changed, some have not, as this extract shows: : 'Our streets are kept clean, and lighted with lamps, every night in the winter season; and so regular are the inhabitants, to their hours of rest, that it is rare to meet any person, after ten or eleven at night ... the common people are very well made and proportioned ... the women are remarkably handsome; it being taken notice of by strangers that they observe more pretty faces in York than in any other place ... the better sort talk the English language in perfection at York. Without the affected tone and mincing speech of the southern people'. He became a member of the Royal Society; debts landed him in a debtor's prison until bailed out by his patron.

## Dukes of York

Usually conferred on the Sovereign's second eldest son, as currently with Prince Andrew, the title has done much to bind York with the monarchy. Edward III' son, Edmund of Langley, was appointed the first Duke of York in 1385 and was founder of the House of York. His father, Edward III, had married **Phillipa of Hainault** in 1328 **in York Minster**. Prince William of Hatfield, a son who died at the age of ten, is buried there in a canopied niche in the North Choir Aisle. Edmund's son Richard took the title from whom it passed to his grandson Richard, Duke of York, whose head was impaled on **Micklegate Bar** as a traitor after the Battle of Wakefield in 1460. In *Henry VI Part III* Shakespeare has Queen Margaret famously say: 'Off with his head and set it on York's gate, so York may overlook the Town of York'. His son, the fourth Duke of York, later Edward IV, defeated Henry VI at the Wars of the Roses Battle of Towton, removed his father's head and replaced it with four Lancastrian heads. In 1920 Prince Albert (son of George V) came to the Minster Chapter House to inaugurate a fund for the Minster glass; at the same time he was presented with the *King's Book of York Fallen Heroes* to be held in perpetuity in the Minster. **E Ridsdale Tate** illuminated the pages and designed the oak boards and silver clasps.

## Duncombe Place

Built between 1860 and 1864 by demolishing buildings on the corner of Blake Street and Lop Lane, or Flea Alley . Duncombe Place was named after Dean Augustus Duncombe in 1858; he himself subscribed £1,000 to help finance the building of the Place. St Wilfrid's Church was completed in 1864.

## Eboracum

The Queen and the Duke of Edinburgh visited York on 28 June 1971 to celebrate the 1,900th anniversary of the founding of York by Roman governor Petilius Cerialis and named **Eboracum** by geographer Ptolemy. The year of celebration began with a New Year's Eve Ball in the **Assembly Rooms** and finished with the December production of Handel's *Messiah* in the **Minster**. Other events included a six day Services Searchlight Tattoo on **Knavesmire** in September; £1 million-worth of military hardware on display on the Knavesmire including a Thunderbird guided missile, a Chieftain tank and a Navy Whirlwind helicopter; a Bootham Park gala with fireworks finale; an exhibition of an Edwardian fair; a 1900th celebration evening race meeting; the Sealed Knot procession and ball; and the cremation of Emperor Severus after a torchlight procession.

## Ebor Day

Part of the four day Yorkshire Ebor Festival traditionally held at the **Knavesmire** in mid-August also featuring Ladies' Day. The Ebor is the oldest (it dates from the 1843) and most famous York race, and the richest handicap in Europe.

## Ebrauk

Mythical founder of York, or **Eoforwic**, in 1010 BC whose statue reputedly stood near **Bootham Bar**.

## Edward III

Married **Philippa of Hainault**, the fifteen-year-old princess in York on 24 January 1328. Edward did much to make York the royal city it is, holding Parliament here seven times between 1328 and 1337.

## The Electric Theatre, Fossgate

One of six **cinemas** in York in 1929. It was opened in 1911, entrance was through an door beneath the screen. From 1951 it was known as the *Scala*; it closed in 1957 and became a furniture shop; the exterior is still beautifully preserved today. Locally it was known as the *Flea Bin* – and a visit meant a 'laugh and scratch'. Admission on Saturday afternoon was 4*d* – or a clean jam jar (an early example of recycling).

## Encore!

The encore had it's premiere in York, at the **Theatre Royal** in 1791 after a performance of the *Conjuror's Song* in which a leg of lamb, a cake and a lawyer in a sack were conjured up. The audience enjoyed this so much that they demanded to see it again – a somewhat difficult request. Performers and orchestra left the stage amid a salvo of candles and candlesticks: the audience was only placated when the orchestra returned to play the song again.

## Eoforwic

The Saxon name for York. Anglo Saxon York was the capital of Deira and then of Deira and Bernicia, later called Northumbria. In the early seventh century, York was an increasingly important city: Paulinus of York ( St Paulinus) established a wooden church here, the forerunner of York **Minster**, in 627; King Edwin of Northumbria was baptised in the same year. Eoforwic, means wild-boar town in Old English; the later Jorvik means horse bay. It is possible that Eoforwice is a later name for Cair Ebrauc, one of the cities mentioned in the *Historia Brittonum* of about 830, founded in legend by **Ebrauk**.

Eoforwic – a scene from the 1909 pageant.

## Etty, William R. A.

The 1911 statue of York artist William Etty (1787-1849) stands proudly outside **York City Art Gallery,** the home of many of his, often controversial and to some, shocking, paintings. Etty founded the York School of Design in 1842, later the York School of Art. We have much to thank him for when it comes to the surviving walls, bars and buildings of York . His sonorous letter to the city's vandals resonates to this day: 'Beware how you destroy your antiquities, guard them with religious care ! They are what give you a decided character and superiority over other provincial cities. You have lost much, take care of what remains.' Etty first exhibited at the Royal Academy in 1811, becoming an Academician in 1828. He is buried in St Olave's, Marygate. The church is named after the patron Saint of Norway, St Olaf.

## Evelyn, W. A.

In 1905 Dr W. A. Evelyn (1860-1935) organized an exhibition in **York City Art Gallery** – *York Views and Worthies,* comprising images of York. He started his famous series of lectures in 1909 and in 1934 he donated his huge collection of pictures to the city to be held in the Gallery. A fervent defender of the city's heritage and member of York Architectural and York Archaeological Society (YAYAS), Dr Evelyn campaigned tirelessly against the destruction or ruination of many of York's finest sights. *The Evelyn Collection* is accessible through YAYAS, www.yayas.free-online.co.uk

## Executions

Between 1370 and 1879 564 convicts were either beheaded or hanged at York. Executions were held on the **Knavesmire** until 1802 when the Grand Jury decided that the 'entrance to the town should no longer be annoyed by dragging criminals through the streets'; the gallows were then transferred to the Castle (The **New Drop**) and then, in 1868, to a scaffold within the **prison** nearby. **Dick Turpin** is, of course, the most notorious Knavesmire, or **Tyburn,** victim. Duke 'Butcher' Cumberland on his victorious return from bloody Culloden left a number of prisoners here to show his gratitude for the city's hospitality: the Sheriff's chaplain read out the message: 'And the Lord said unto Moses "Take all the heads of the people and hang them up before the sun"'. Twenty-three were duly left to hang for ten minutes, stripped and quartered, their heads stuck on **Micklegate Bar.** Cumberland Street was named after the butcher Duke.

## Fairfax House

One of the finest Georgian town houses in England, Fairfax House was originally the winter home of Viscount Fairfax having been purchased in 1760 as a dowry to Anne Fairfax . Its richly decorated interior was redesigned in the classical style by York architect **John Carr** with its magnificent staircase, ceilings, Venetian window and iron balusters. Adapted in the last century for use as a **cinema** and dance hall, Fairfax House was restored to its former glory by York Civic Trust in 1982-84. Sir Simon Jenkins said of it in 2003 'it is the most perfect eighteenth century townhouse I have come across anywhere in England.' The **Noel Terry** collection of furniture, clocks, paintings and decorative arts, described by Christie's as one of the finest private collections of the twentieth century, furnish the house.

### Fawkes, Guy

Fawkes was born just off Low Petergate, baptised at St Michael le Belfry and a pupil at **St Peter's**. As Captain Guido Fawkes he had a distinguished military record, and his expertise with explosives led the Plotters to recruit him in their attempt to assassinate James I. Guy Fawkes, calling himself Johnson, a servant to Thomas Percy, smuggled thirty-six barrels of gunpowder under the House of Lords, ready for its royal opening on 5 November 1605. Just before midnight he was arrested, 'booted and spurred', ready to make his get-away, having on his person a watch, lantern, tinder-box and slow fuses. He was interviewed by King James in his bedchamber, taken to the Tower to be tortured, and finally 'hanged, drawn and quartered' as a traitor on 31 January 1606. Though he is still burnt in effigy on 5 November ('Plot Night' as it is called in parts of Yorkshire) no Guy is ever burnt at St Peter's.

### Fiennes, Celia

The intrepid lady traveller journeyed the length and breadth of the country, often with only one or two maids in attendance; she visited York in 1697. This is how she described the **River 'Ouise'** and the mean streets of York in her journal *Great Journey to Newcastle and to Cornwall*: 'it bears Great Barges, it Looks muddy, its full of good ffish. We Eate very good Cod fish and Salmon and that at a pretty Cheape rate, tho' we were not in the best jnn for the Angel is the best in Cunny Streete. The houses are very Low and as jndifferent as in any Country town and the Narrowness of y^e Streetes makes it appear very mean'.

### Fishergate Bar

Sometimes called St George's Bar, this is the gateway to Selby; chains ran across the **River Foss** here to the castle to reinforce York's defences. The bar was blocked in 1489 after rebels damaged it in protest at punitive taxation (fire damage is still visible); it was eventually reopened in 1827 to allow access to the **Cattle Market**. In Elizabethan times it was a prison for rascals and lunatics.

### Fishergate Postern

The three storey Fishergate Postern (previously the Talkan Tower) – *posternam iuxta Skarletpit* – dates from 1502 and is York's only surviving example. Buildings adjoining the postern were destroyed in a 1489 riot. The tower was originally called Edward's tower. A projecting lavatory discharged into the adjacent King's Pool. **Dick Turpin's** grave is nearby in the garden on the site of St George's church. He was executed on 7 April 1739 after spending time in a cell which can still be seen in the Debtor's Prison in the **Castle Museum**.

### Flambeaux Extinguishers

Before gas and electricity it was a legal requirement in York for the pedestrian to carry 'light before him'. On reaching his or her destination they would put out their torches in the extinguishers located in door niches. Three survive in York: at the **Red House**, in Gillygate and in Petergate.

## The Foss Navigation

The River **Foss** was canalised by the Foss Navigation Company as far as the bridge at Sheriff Hutton in 1806, a thriving town then. It cost £35,000; 1809 provided the best toll receipts: £1,384. Up cargoes included lime for the local agricultural industry and other materials for the tannery in Strensall, and coal. Goods coming back to York were hay, oats, cheeses, manure and other agricultural produce. The horses that hauled the barges could manage a weight of twenty-seven tons given a favourable current; the same horse could cope with only one ton road cargo. The opening of the York to Scarborough **railway** through Haxby and Strensall in 1845 and the York to Hull line through Huntington in 1847 rendered the canal commercially redundant in 1852 – the first navigation to close as a result of the railways.

## Freemen

To trade in York it was necessary to be a Freeman and to join one of the eighty or so guilds associated with one's trade. *The Freemens Rolls* date from 1272: the Freemen were responsible for civil and criminal justice, controlled the guilds, supervised the training of apprentices and the quality of goods. They kept the streets clean, kept the city walls in good order, maintained roads and bridges, built schools, were the first to be called to arms and provided troops for the monarch. It was the Freemen who collected the taxes for the king or queen and who implemented the civic democracy in York, as bestowed by King John in 1212 and celebrated in 2012 by York 800. Franchise could be bought – at the high price of £25 in the eighteenth century. John Moore is the only black man on the *Rolls* – bluntly, albeit accurately, listed as John Moore – 'black'.

## Friaries

Up until the Dissolution York had at least five friaries. The Carmelites came to York in the early 1250s, setting up first in **Bootham** (outside the walls). In about 1295 they established themselves between Fossgate and **Hungate**. The Franciscans arrived here around 1230; their site was between the **castle** and **Ouse Bridge** in Tower Place. In 1299 there were fifty-two friars; the importance of the friary can be shown by the fact that Edward II, Edward III and Richard II all stayed there. A section of the wall is still visible. The Dominicans arrived in about 1226 and set up the King's Chapel of St Mary Magdalene around Toft Green; early in the fourteenth century there were up to sixty friars, including John Wycliffe in the 1350s. Henry III allowed them forty oak trees from the Forest of Galtres and in 1268 permitted them to enclose land which included a public well so long as they established an alternative one for the public to use. The Augustinians had arrived from Tickhill by 1272. Their friary was between Lendal and the river; by 1300 there were thirty-five friars. A catalogue of its library has survived from 1372, listing 646 items. In 1854 the gateway to the Alien Benedictine Priory in Micklegate was demolished to make way for the building of **Priory Street**.

## Friends' Burial Ground, Bishophill

In keeping with Quaker practice the graves here are all very simple and describe only the age of the deceased and the date of death, so as not 'to exalt the creature'. Months are given in numerals only; there are two reasons for this: firstly the names we use celebrate pagan gods and, secondly, where this is not the case they are sometimes wrong, as in the case of December which is not the tenth month. Notable denizens include Lindley Murray (d.1726) and **William Tuke**. Murray was author of *The English Grammar*, published in 1795 for staff and pupils of the Girl's Friend's School (later the **Mount**). The book went into 170 editions, the last of which was published in the USA in 1871. A new Quaker burial ground opened in Heslington Road in 1855.

## Friends' Meeting House

Between **Castlegate** and **Clifford Street**; the facade is from 1885 although the interior goes back to 1815. **Quakers** have no ministers: they meet in silence, broken only when a member of the congregation feels moved to speak – 'spoken ministry'.

## F. R. Stubbs, Ironmongers

The Stubbs sign on the wall of its grand old five storey, thirty-seven room building is as famous locally as the *Bile Beans* ghost advertisement in Lord Mayor's Walk. Established in 1904 by Francis Stubbs in **Lady Peckett's Yard** the business (mainly suppliers to the trade) moved to its present Grade II listed building in 1915, Foss Bridge House built in 1878. Stubb's slogan was 'Better Buy on the Bridge'. In 2001 it was bought by Loch Fyne Restaurants.

Challengers – the home of Fulford Biscuits.

## Fulford Biscuits

Fulford Biscuits in Coppergate and Heslington Road was run by Misses A. and F. Challenger; they had brought their confectionery skills from Sheffield and Harrogate and bought the sole rights to produce the famous, secret recipe Fulford Biscuit from the estate of the late Mrs G. Leng. The Leng business had been set up in the 1820s and won prizes at the Leeds Exhibition in 1868 and the York Exhibition in 1866. In her *Good Things in England* (1932) Florence White says that they 'tasted like a mixture of a Bath Oliver and plain water biscuit ... and they were delicious' – perhaps because they were always sold fresh.

## Fulford Cavalry Barracks

Built in 1796 the barracks were initially very unpopular amongst the troops because horse manure was routinely piled up outside the men's windows and there were no latrines for nocturnal use. The adjacent Infantry Barracks were built between 1877 and 1880, at a cost of £15,000. In 1951 the barracks were renamed Imphal Barracks after the West Yorkshire Regiment's brave defence of Imphal Plain, Burma, in June 1944. Today it is home to HQ York Garrison, 15 (NE) Brigade HQ, 2 Signal Regiment and the Defence Vetting Agency.

## Fulford Open Air School

Originally opened at 11 Castlegate in 1913 in the same building as the Tuberculosis Dispensary; it moved in 1914 to a converted army hut in the grounds of Fulford House and became known as Fulford Road School for Delicate and Partially Sighted Children. The open air school movement was set up in 1904 in Berlin to curb the development of tuberculosis in children and, as such, required the establishment of schools that combine medical care with teaching adapted to pupils with pre-tuberculosis. Fulford closed in 1960 and was demolished in 1964. The Holgate Bridge School for Mentally Defective Boys was opened in 1911 and moved to Fulford House, later known as Fulford Road School for Educationally Sub-Normal Children, in 1923.

### The Gazebo on the Minster
Odd as it may seem there was an hexagonal shaped gazebo on the lantern tower of York **Minster** from 1666 to 1808. It was built there on the instructions of George Villiers, Duke of Buckingham and Lord Lieutenant of West Yorkshire and the City of York, to house a beacon which would be lit in the event of an invasion by the Dutch or French, our enemies in 1666. Made of wood and glass and covered in lead it had a cockerel weather vane on top which symbolized St Peter.

### Gent, Thomas
Irishman, author, publisher and **printer**. A contemporary review described his work 'for the most part below mediocrity, yet they possess a certain quaintness and eccentricity of character which are not without their charm'. Be that as it may, Gent's books on York, Hull and Ripon are still much sought after. He worked for printer **John White,** marrying in to the family and inheriting the business which made him York's only typographer for a while and proprietor of the 1719 *York Mercury* from 1724.

The eccentric Thomas Gent from a mezzotinto engraving by Valentine Green, after Nathan Drake.

Outside The George in Coney Street during the races as the London coach pulls up. Some things never change.

## The George Hotel

One of York's coaching inns serving Hull, Manchester and Newcastle in Coney Street opposite the **Black Swan** and the *York Courant* until 1869 when the inn was tragically knocked down to make way for Leak & Thorp. In 1867 it was called *Winn's George Hotel*. There was an earlier inn on the site called *The Bull*: the landlord, Thomas Kaye, replaced this with *The George* in 1614. Famous guests included Anne and Charlotte Bronte in May 1849 en route to Scarborough; they shopped and visited the Minster. Four days later Anne died of consumption aged twenty-nine.

## Gillygate

Gillygate was originally called 'Invico Sancti Egidi', then Giligate in 1373 after St Giles Church. The church was demolished in 1547; the Salvation Army citadel opened by General Booth in 1882 now stands on the site. Clarence Street houses and nearby Union Street car park were built on land in 1835 called the Horsefair; three horse fairs were held here every year.

## The Glassworks

The first glassworks was opened in 1794 by Hampston and Prince near Fishergate making flint glass and medicinal phials. The York Flint Glass Company was set up in 1835 and by 1851 was a bigger employer than either **Terry** or **Craven**. In 1930 it was incorporated as National Glass Works (York) Ltd which became Redfearn National Glass Company in 1967; demolished in 1988 it is replaced by the Novotel. Sand for the works came via the Foss Islands Branch Line Depot; the line (operational from 1879 to 1988) also served the electricity power station and **cattle market**.

## Godfrey, Thomas, Bookseller and Phrenologist

Thomas Godfrey was a phrenologist who invented his qualifications; he opened his first bookshop at 46½ Stonegate in 1895 selling second hand books 'recently purchased from private libraries'. The business was called 'Ye Olde Boke Shoppe' but it failed: Godfrey 'became dissatisfied of the apathy of the citizens and disposed of the business' – sentiments and actions which could be echoed by many an independent bookseller today. An alternative report, though, attributes his failure to the selling of Oscar Wilde's *Portrait of Dorian Gray* after it had been recalled by the publishers thus giving 'offence to some of the good people in York by his handling of a book which was regarded at the time as a most indecent publication'. Godfrey tried again in 1904 at 37 Goodramgate with the Eclectic Book Company, eventually moving back to 16 Stonegate with a business imaginatively named The Book Company, later Edward S. Pickard. In 1982 the business moved over the road to 32 Stonegate and acquired a second shop on the campus at **York University**.

## The Golden Fleece

The ancient *Golden Fleece* still survives (with its impressive golden sheep hanging above the door) on Pavement – as does the fifteenth-century timber framed Tudor mansion in the centre, once the home of **Thomas Herbert**, Bart. born there in 1606. To the right is **Rowntree's** shop; members of the family lived above. The pub is reputedly haunted, home to no fewer than seven ghosts. Earliest mention is in the City Archive of 1503; it originally belonged to **The Merchant Adventurers'** who named it to celebrate their thriving woollen trade. In 1702, John Peckett, **Lord Mayor** owned it. The building has no foundations which accounts in part for its lop-sidedness.

Goodramgate before the link road to Deangate.

## Goodramgate

Named after Guthrum, a Danish chief active around 878. In 1901 York **Minster** gave permission for Deangate to pass close to the South Transept, linking Goodramgate with Duncombe Place and High Petergate. In time this led to over 2,000 vehicles per hour passing close to the Minster. It was closed to traffic in 1991.

## Goodricke, John

Born in Groningen on 17 September 1764 and lived most of his life at the **Treasurer's House**; at the age of five he contracted scarlet fever which left him profoundly deaf and dumb. Notwithstanding, Goodricke became an accomplished astronomer; the plaque outside his home reads: 'From a window in the Treasurer's House, City of York, the young deaf and dumb astronomer John Goodrick, who was elected a fellow of the Royal Society at the age of twenty-one, observed the periodicity of the star ALGOL and discovered the variation of CEPHEL and other stars thus laying the foundation of modern measurement of the Universe.' He died, aged twenty-one. His cousin was Edward Piggott (1753-1825), another gifted York astronomer who worked with Goodricke in their observatory behind the Black Horse Inn in **Bootham**.

## Grand Opera House

The buildings that today house the Grand Opera House were never intended to be a theatre. The tall section was built as York's Corn Exchange in 1868 with plans to use it

John Cleese at the Grand Opera House, 2011.

occasionally as a concert hall. The auditorium was originally a warehouse opening onto Kings Street. In 1902 when the Corn Exchange failed, the buildings were converted by William Peacock. The theatre opened on 20 January 1902 with *Little Red Riding Hood* starring Florrie Ford. In 1903 the name was changed to The Grand Opera House and Empire because new regulations banned smoking in theatres but permitted it in music halls. It stayed with William Peacock's family until 1945; performers included Charlie and Sydney Chaplin, Gracie Fields, Lillie Langtry, George Robey, Cecily Courtneidge and Jimmy Jewel. From 1945 to 1956 F. J. Butterworth owned the theatre and stars such as Vera Lynn, Laurel and Hardy and Morecome and Wise appeared. In 1958 Shepherd of the **Shambles** bought it, and it became the SS *Empire*. The stage, lower boxes and raked stall floor were removed and replaced by a large flat floor suitable for roller-skating, dancing, bingo and wrestling. In 1987 new owners the India Pru Co. Ltd spent £4,000,000 restoring it to its former glory.

## Grand Yorkshire Gala

Ascents in hot air balloons were a regular feature at the annual gala held in the grounds of **Bootham Park Hospital** (which became known as Gala Fields) from 1858 to 1923. One year one of the balloons broke its moorings and took its eight passengers on an unexpected, albeit short, ride. Other attractions included military bands, roundabouts, helter-skelter: Holdsworth's Alpine Glassade – 'Why go to Switzerland?' 'Ladies Specially Invited'; evening firework displays, acrobatics, juggling and shooting galleries. So popular was it that it became a three day event and seriously depressed attendances at York races when they coincided. The gala moved to Fulford in 1924 and then to the **Knavesmire**.

## Gray's Court

Grays Court is probably the oldest continuously occupied house in the country; parts of it date back to 1080 when it was commissioned by the first Norman **Archbishop of York**, Thomas de Bayeux. Grays Court was the original **Treasurers House**. It exudes history: James I dined here with Edmund, Lord Sheffield, the Lord President of the North, knighting eight noblemen in the Long Gallery in one evening. Sir Thomas Fairfax owned Grays Court between 1649 and 1663 during which time he laid siege to the city. James Duke of York and Maria Beatrix of Modena, his wife, later King and Queen, stayed in Grays Court in 1679. Elizabeth Robinson was born here in 1718: she founded the Blue-stocking Club 'where literary topics were to be discussed, but politics, gossip and card-playing were barred'.

## Great Peter

The 10.8 ton Great Peter arrived back at a York Minster in 1914 after restoration; ten horses were required to pull the cart. The bell was originally cast by John Taylor & Co of Loughborough in 1840 and is Britain's second biggest bell after Great Paul – which Taylor's also cast (9 feet high and weighing seventeen tons) and hangs in St Paul's Cathedral. Great Peter is the heaviest of the Minster's ring of twelve bells but, despite its weight, can be swung and rung by one person. It is the deepest-toned bell in

Europe. Taylors was established in 1784 and still trades today. The bells were restored and returned here in March 1914 by John Warner & Sons Ltd from their Spitalfields Bell Foundry. The **Minster** can boast thirty-five bells in total. The north-west tower contains Great Peter and six clock bells (the largest weighing three tons). The south-west tower houses 14 bells (tenor is 3 tons) hung and rung for change ringing and twenty-two carillon bells (tenor 1.2 tons) which are played from a baton keyboard in the ringing chamber.

## Guildhall

The hall was built in 1445 on the site of the earlier 'Common Hall' dating from at least 1256. It was originally for the Guild of St Christopher and St George and the Corporation who took over completely in 1549. Council meetings are still held there in the Victorian Council Chamber of 1891. It was used as a theatre – **Richard III** watched *Credo* here in 1483 – and as a Court of Justice, and was where **Margaret Clitherow** was tried in 1586. In 1647 during the Civil War, Cromwell agreed to pay a ransom of £200,000 to the Scots in exchange for Charles I; the money was counted here. It contains a bell captured at the Siege of Rangoon in 1851. The Guildhall was badly damaged in the **Baedeker Raid** of 1942 but fully restored in 1960. The subterranean Common Hall Lane passes under the Guildhall – then called Common Hall, to a jetty on the river, originally a continuation of **Stonegate**.

## Hainault Riots

In 1327 60,000 or so troops were stationed in York in preparation for war against the Scots. The garrison included allied troops from Hainault and Zeeland, many of whom were slain by the English when skirmishes broke out. Hostilities resumed in 1329 during the festivities for the marriage of **Edward III** and **Philippa of Hainault** in York: 242 English and 347 Hainaulters died on the banks of the **Ouse**.

## Hansom, Joseph

Joseph Aloysius Hansom (1842-1900), the architect and inventor of the Patent Safety Cabriolet that bears his name, was born at 114 **Micklegate** and christened in the Bar **Convent** chapel. He suffered from severe depression and shot himself in his office on 27 May 1900. A pub in Market Street is named after him. Architecturally, Hansom's best known work is probably the majestic neoclassical Birmingham Town Hall. The Hansom Cab was so common a sight that Disraeli called it 'the gondola of London'.

## Hargrove, William

Son of Ely, bookseller and publisher of Knaresborough. William (d. 1862) was a prominent historian and author of the invaluable *History and Description of the Ancient City of York* (1818) and the *New Guide for Strangers and Residents of the City of York* (1838). William bought the **York Herald** in 1813 and edited it until 1848 from the York City & County Library in **Coney Street** next to **St Martin-le-Grand**. His son, Alfred Hargrove, was the author of *The Baneful Custom of Interment in Towns* which included descriptions of York's baneful cemeteries.

Harker's Hotel.

## Harker's Hotel

Built on the site of *The York Tavern* in 1770, Harker's was named after a butler who had worked at *The Tavern*. It was pulled down in 1928 so that St Helen's Square could be widened (it used to be triangular). Harker's then decamped to Dringhouses; a 1929 advertisement claimed it to be 'The best and most up to date hotel in the city.' The name lives on in the Square though: *Harker's Bar* now occupies the grand Yorkshire Insurance Company building which opened in 1924. *The York Tavern* was a coaching house with room for 150 horses.

## The Herald

The four page *York Herald and County Advertiser* was first published in 1790 in High Ousegate. Soon it was making net profits of up to £1,500 and moved from weekly publication to daily in 1874 by which time it was printed in Coney Street at the former office of the **York Courant**. In 1890 it became the *Yorkshire Herald*, and eventually increased to eight pages.

## Herbert, Sir Thomas

Charles I's groom of the royal bedchamber; he was with the king at his execution until he was 'to the horror of all the world, brought to the block'. Charles II made him a baronet for his services. Herbert was a great traveller and visited the Shah of Persia in the 1620s; the Shah presented him with a full Persian costume and a black page boy – both feature in a portrait of Herbert. The house in **Pavement** which inaccurately bears his name was built by John Jaques in 1614 who had bought property from Sir Thomas' great grandfather, Christopher Herbert. Thomas Herbert died at home in 1682 in Petergate.

Heslington Hall.

## Heslington Hall

Lord Deramore was the Lord of the Manor during the 1930s, owner of Heslington Hall, later to become part of the **University of York** in the 1960s. It was built between in 1568 for Sir Thomas Eynns, secretary to the Council in the North (1550-78). Sir Thomas Hesketh, owner of Castle Mills, built an **almshouse** hospital in the grounds for eight poor men and one woman; when the Foss Navigation Company bought the Mills in 1793 they agreed to pay the hospital £50 pa in perpetuity, a sum which is still paid today. In 1795 Henry Yarburgh rebuilt the hospital on Heslington Lane. During the Second World War it was requisitioned as Headquarters of 64 Group, Bomber Command.

## Holgate Mill

The imposing 1770 five-sail mill built on the site of a fifteenth-century predecessor. At that time Holgate was a village with a population of fifty-five. Unusually the mill had five double-shuttered sails; they were damaged in a 1930 storm and taken down after which time the mill was powered by an electric motor. The Holgate Windmill Preservation Society looks after the mill today and completed a marvellous reconstruction in 2012.

## Holy Trinity Church, Micklegate

Richard II visited in 1397; the tower collapsed in 1552. There are ancient stocks in the church and a memorial to Dr **John Burton**, historian and model for Dr Slop in Sterne's *Life & Times of Tristram Shandy, Gentleman*. The oldest part is the nave of a former late-eleventh-century Benedictine Priory. The ornate doorway was removed to Ingram's **almshouses**.

## Hospitals

York was nothing if not well served by hospitals in the Middle Ages, with at least thirty-one. The most important, and biggest, was **St Leonard's**. One of the earliest was St Nicholas' **leper hospital**. St Giles in Gillygate, was set up before 1274. There was a hospital at **Ouse Bridge** in the thirteenth century, a Maison Dieu, originally catering for the poor and lepers. **St Mary's** Hospital was in Bootham.

## The Hospitium

This fine fourteenth-century half-timbered building in **Museum Gardens** was probably designed both as a guest house for visitors to the nearby **St Mary's Abbey** and as a warehouse for goods unloaded from the river nearby. There was an Elizabethan knot garden with central fountain between the Hospitium and the river.

## House of York

The descendents of Edmund of Langley, the first **Duke of York**, fifth son of **Edward III** and protagonists in the Wars of the Roses.

## Houses of Correction

There were two in York: one on **Old Baile** from 1807, the other on **Toft Green** from 1814. The provision of a tread-wheel seems to have exercised the authorities for some time before one was installed in 1825 – 'a terror to evil-doers'. A typical wheel would have been 5 feet in diameter with twenty-four steps holding twenty-four convicts taking forty-five steps per minute for ten hours in the summer and seven in winter. The (often disregarded) maximum was limited to 12,000 feet in ascent in one day or just under 3 miles. Many simply 'ground air' but at Toft Green the authorities found a commercial angle when they used it in an adjacent bone house for (animal) bone crushing. Unfortunately the wheel here was often used as a ladder of escape necessitating its removal from the wall; it was taken away completely in 1833 and prisoners reverted to smashing boulders.

## Howard, Catherine

Fifth wife of Henry VIII, she came with him to York in 1541 and allegedly consummated her affair with Thomas Culpepper in the rose garden of the **King's Manor**. Jane Seymour was destined to be crowned Queen in the **Minster** but died giving birth to Edward VI in 1537.

## Howard, Ebenezer

In developing **New Earswick**, **Joseph Rowntree** was heavily influenced by Ebenezer Howard's (1850-1928) vision of a kind of utopian city where citizens lived in harmony with nature, as expounded in his 1898 *Tomorrow: A Peaceful Path to Real Reform*, retitled *Garden Cities of Tomorrow* in 1902. Howard's towns were to be slum free, and managed and financed by the residents who had a financial interest. They combined the best of town and country life. Equal opportunity, good wages, entertainment, low rents, beauty, fresh air were the aim and we can recognise all of these factors in Joseph Rowntree's New Earswick. Howard's humanism and progressive vision was influential in other countries too, not least in Germany where the German Garden City Association, '*unseren Deustschen Vettern*' as the people of the village welcomed them on their visit in 1909, flourished. There is, however, a sinister side to the story. Theodor Fritsch (1852-1933) claimed to be the originator of the garden city concept, anticipating Howard in his 1896 *Die Stadt der Zukunft (The City of the Future)*, the 1912 second edition of which was subtitled *Gartenstad (Garden City)*. Fritsch took a highly racist perspective – completely at odds with Howard's – that later contributed to Nazi ideology and made Fritsch something of a prophet of Nazism. His other work, largely published in his journal, *Hammer*, was anti-Semitic and supremacist. Despite the fact that in 1910 German eugenicists were sitting on the board of the GGCA and the long tradition of town planning and architecture being hijacked in the name of racial cleansing and eugenics, the Association rejected Fritsch. This did not, however, stop the establishment in Bremen of a *siedlung* under the Third Reich: part garden city, part half-open prison, part eugenicistic selection centre.

## Howerd, Frankie

Francis Alick Howerd, master of the camp and the *double entendre* was born in York in 1917 at 53 Hartoft Street, Fulford Road; a wall plaque at the **Grand Opera House** celebrates his life which ended in 1992. His mother worked at **Terry's.**

## Hudson, George

York's 'Railway King' who advised George Stephenson to make all the trains come through York, rather than Leeds. Hudson was **Lord Mayor** from 1837-1839. His use of public money, though worthy, was questionable: he laid on 'an excellent and substantial breakfast' for poor citizens to celebrate Victoria's coronation in 1838 and doled out free food coupons for 14,000 of the 'lower orders'. By 1846 he was involved in railway projects to the tune of £10 million and was elected Tory MP for Sunderland: his companies controlled more than 25 per cent of England's railways. He was chairman of the York, Newcastle and Berwick Railway and, in 1854, the North Eastern Railway, before being disgraced when dubious share dealings were uncovered by **George Leeman** and others. He was expelled from the city council in 1849 , and his effigy at *Madame Tussauds* was ignominiously melted down. After a period of exile in Calais he stood for the Whitby parliamentary seat in 1865 (vacant on the death of George Stephenson) but was arrested before the election and jailed for three months at York. He died in London, a pauper, in 1871.

George Hudson, on the left, meeting Queen Victoria and Prince Albert – their expressions may reveal something about what the future held for the Railway King – as featured in the 1971 Pageant of York.

## Hungate

Hungate derives from Hundgate – street of the dogs – a common Viking street name. As a result of **Seebohm Rowntree's** *Poverty* in 1908 and 1914 York's medical officer, Edmund Smith, produced reports condemning streets in Hungate and Walmgate as unfit for habitation; 'The back yards in Hope Street and Albert Street and in some other quarters can only be viewed with repulsion – they are so small and fetid, and so hemmed-in by surrounding houses and other buildings… There are no amenities; it is an absolute slum.' At the 1921 census York's population was 84052 with 18608 inhabited houses (= 4.5 persons per dwelling).

## The Ice House

This brick-lined vaulted early nineteenth-century edifice is on the city walls near **Monkgate Bar**; it was used for the storage of winter ice which, in turn, would be used for the cooling and preservation of food and drink in the summer.

## The Industrial Ragged School

The school was founded in 1848, moving from College Street into the Marygate premises vacated by the **workhouse**. In 1855, an average of eighty children attended the school in winter and forty in summer. The boys were taught clog-making, tailoring, gardening, and net-making, the girls were instructed in domestic work and needlework. They all received three meals a day and some boarded and were occasionally sent out to work. By 1876, it had become a Certified Industrial School for Boys continuing until 1921.

Poverty in Hungate in the early twentieth century.

## Instruments of Torture

In June 1899 an advertisement appeared in the *Yorkshire Herald* for what promised to be a riveting night out: 'A series of lectures upon object lessons, consisting of actual instruments of torture now sanctioned by the Roman Church used by the Romanizing clergy'. Exhibits included a 'Spiked Iron Cage from the Kilburn Sisterhood, used for the Incarceration of Children in their Orphanages; hair Shirts, Rope, Steel Whips, Armlets, steel with sharp points, Cinctures'. Admission was free; questions were invited; lectures were given by ... members of the Protestant Alliance.

## Jacob's Well

A fifteenth-century timber-framed house in Trinity Lane off Micklegate; it became an inn from 1750 to 1903 called *The Jacob's Well*. The unusual fifteenth-century canopy over the door was taken from *The Wheatsheaf* in **Davygate**, at one time the residence of the Bishops of Durham.

## Jewbury

The result of Henry II's 1177 edict that every city should have a **Jewish** burial ground without the city walls – before that the deceased were transported to London for burial.

## The Jewish Massacre

Jews settled in York from about 1175. As Christians were forbidden to lend money (usury) Jews frequently provided this service. The massacre started in 1190 at Westminster during the coronation of Richard I where Jews bearing gifts were excluded and fatally attacked. One of the victims was Benedict of York; his colleague Jocenus returned home to find that the unrest had spread to York. Misunderstandings between the Sheriff and the constable led to an anti Semitic mob of debtors and crusaders attacking 150 or so Jews. They took refuge in York **castle** where, poorly provisioned, they were besieged by the people of York. Rather than capitulate to either death or forced baptism they committed mass suicide by cutting throats and setting fire to the castle. The survivors were murdered and all the records of debts to Jews were stolen and burnt.

## King John

King John, brother of Richard the Lionheart, awarded York its charter in 1212, 801 years ago, and signed the *Magna Carta* in 1215 with Walter de Grey, **Archbishop of York**.

## Jorvik

The Viking name for York. The Viking army attacked the city on 1 November 866 under the command of Halfdan and Ivar the Boneless. The date was no coincidence, it being All Saints' Day when much of the population would have been preoccupied in the old cathedral. York soon became the capital of the Viking kingdom in the north. In 954 the last Viking king, Eric Bloodaxe was expelled. Ivar was boneless on account of his chubby face; he was the son of Ragnar Lothbrok.

## Jorvik Viking Centre

The only significant archaeological finds in York before the 1970s were dug up by chance. But this all changed when an area below Lloyds Bank in **Pavement** was excavated by York Archaeological Trust before the redevelopment of Coppergate in 1976: within days rare traces of **Viking** Age timber buildings were revealed. The dig covered 1000 square metres and so between 1976 and 1981 archaeologists were able to excavate 2000 years of York's history. In that time York Archaeological Trust identified and recorded around 40,000 items. The site revealed: five tons of animal bones – mostly food leftovers consumed over the centuries; vast quantities of oyster shells – a cheap and popular food over the years; thousands of **Roman** and mediaeval roof tiles; building materials including wattle, timber and metal slag; 250,000 pieces of pottery; 20,000 other individually interesting objects. Many of the Viking artefacts are on display here along with a vibrant reconstruction of Viking life.

## Joseph Rowntree Memorial Library

**Joseph Rowntree's** enlightened attitude to industrial relations showed itself in many ways: in 1885 he stocked and opened a library for his workers putting in £10 matched by a grant from the company's Pure Literature Society. There were originally three

The Joseph Rowntree School.

libraries: the Staff Library held 10,000 books, half of which were fiction, 4,000 non-fiction and 1,000 juvenile. The Lad's Library had 250 books for the Boy's Club and the Technical Library kept 7,000 books and 8,000 pamphlets as well as having 300 subscriptions to magazines and journals. The Joseph Rowntree Memorial Library was erected in 1927 in Haxby Road in gratitude for a life of devoted service; another example of cultural philanthropy is the famous Rowntree Theatre over the road.

## Joseph Rowntree School
The first Joseph Rowntree secondary School was opened on 12 January 1942 by Rab Butler to cater for 480 children (in classes of forty) from age eleven from the village and surrounding area. As with the primary school it was nothing if not innovative for its time, taking advice, for example, from the National Institute of Industrial Psychology on ergonomic matters such as ventilation, heating and lighting. From the very start practical skills were valued and taught in equal measure to academic subjects. Printing and typography were part of the curriculum, a reflection perhaps of the traditional importance of **printing** and publishing in York, with companies like Sessions just down the road in Huntington. Adult education was encouraged too, in line with the **Rowntree** philosophy, with an Evening Institute of 350 students.

## Joseph Rowntree Trusts
The 1904 Trust is now in fact four Trusts: the Memorial Trust (the Village Trust); the Charitable Trust, the Reform Trust and the Foundation. The objective of the first was to bring to life the idea of the new garden village, **New Earswick,** which was to provide the worker of even the lowest means a new type of house that was clean, sanitary and

efficient. It lives on today as Joseph Rowntree Housing Trust which provides housing, retirement care and adult services. The Charitable Trust gives grants to promote peace, equality and accountability; the Reform Trust 'aims to correct imbalances of political power, strengthening the hands of individuals and organisations striving for reform'. The Foundation encourages social change for people and places in poverty, to build communities where everyone can thrive in a more equal society.

## Jubbergate

Originally Joubrettagate – the Street of the Bretons in the **Jewish** Quarter – and Jubretgate. Over the years occupants have included Webster's kitchen and bath-ware shop which became Pawson's, specialists in rubber-ware; *The White Rose Inn* which became Forrington's furnishers around 1920. At one stage in its life it was home to six families. Jubbergate originally extended to cover what is today Market Street as far as **Coney Street**. York's first police station was here until 1880 when it moved to **Clifford Street**.

## Judges' Lodgings

A fine Georgian town house in Lendal, and a good place to stay for the judiciary attending the assizes convenient as it was for the **Assembly Rooms** and **Terry's Restaurant,** from which breakfasts were delivered each morning. The Lodgings is on the site of a late Roman interval tower and was built in 1726 for Dr Wintringham (d. 1748), a very eminent doctor and Physician at York **County Hospital** in 1746. An effigy of Aesculapius guards the door. Wintringham has a monument in his memory at Westminster Abbey; he is buried in St Michael-le-Belfrey. When the Judges were in residence they took an official breakfast on day one at the **Mansion House** as guests of the **Lord Mayor,** to which they would process in their wigs and robes. It was the official judges' residence until 1976.

## Kidcotes

A colloquial name for a prison, two of which were on the old **Ouse Bridge**. The Sheriff ran one for felons; the **Archbishop** the other for drunks and harlots. **Margaret Clitherow** was held here before her trial.

## Kill Canon Corner

The area around the west front of the **Minster** – notorious for its powerful eddying winds.

## The King's Manor

This marvellous, often overlooked, building off Exhibition Square, was originally built in 1270 as the house of the Abbott at **St Mary's Abbey.** It was rebuilt in 1480: the new windows providing the earliest known examples of the use of terracotta as a building material. In 1561 after the Dissolution the Lord President of the Northern Council took possession. Visitors included Henry VIII and James I; during the Siege of York in 1644 it was the Royalists' headquarters. The ornate doorway with the stunning coat of arms at the main entrance is Jacobean; the 'IR' stands for James I who ordered the Manor be converted into a royal palace for him to stay in to and from London and Edinburgh. Charles I added the royal arms, celebrating the Stuarts. After a long period of private lettings, and decay, Mr Lumley's Boarding School for Ladies occupied it from 1712-1835 and then the William Wilberforce inspired Yorkshire **School for the Blind** moved in in 1833 and from the 1870s gradually restored and enlarged the buildings, adding a gymnasium and a cloister to create a second courtyard. The Blind School left in 1958; the Manor was then acquired by York City Council, who leased it to the **University of York** in 1963.

## The King's Fishpool
Around the **Red Tower**, created when the Normans dammed the **River Foss**. It was variously described as 'the disgrace of York ... a stinking morass' and by **Francis Drake** as the repository for 'any dung of beasts or other nastinesses'. The Corporation drained it in 1854 and built Foss Islands Road.

## King's Square
The **Roman** Porta Principalis Sinistra, King's Square was home to Holy Trinity Church before it was demolished in 1935. It was traditionally the Butcher's Church on account of its proximity to **Shambles**. A projecting chapel known as Langton's Chantry was York's first fire station.

## The King's Touch
The practice whereby the reigning monarch touched his or her subjects as a form of medical treatment; in 1639 Charles I 'touched' 200 people in York. In England and France it was believed that a royal touch could heal scrofula or the 'king's evil' – a swelling of the lymph nodes in the neck caused by tuberculosis. It began with Edward the Confessor (1003-1066) and Philip I (1052-1108) of France. The 'royal touch' illustrated the monarch's divine right to rule. Those touched received special gold coins called 'touchpieces' often used as amulets.

## The Knavesmire
The largest and best known of York's strays Micklegate Stray, or the Knavesmire as it is popularly known, has long been a focus for entertainment – from public **executions** to horse racing today. Grazing horses and cattle were a common sight on the Knavesmire from the early nineteenth century through to the 1960s, originally because local householders held grazing rights here and because grazing was the traditional way of managing the pasture. York Races moved to the Knavesmire in 1731 from flood-prone Clifton, sometimes attracting crowds of over 100,000. The races were accompanied by sideshows, gypsy bands and cock fights, and **executions** at York's **Tyburn.** They were timed to follow the assizes in August, when the gentry were in town for court business and when death sentences were handed down. The dawn of aviation was a time of few suitable landing places, so the racecourse and surrounding land was an obvious choice when the army needed to land at York. After the German bombardment of Hartlepool,

Parliament Street in the 1940s.

Scarborough and Whitby in December 1914, 33 Squadron was stationed here, causing much anger amongst local residents fearing that their presence would attract bombing raids to York. In the event, the city was bombed by **Zeppelin** L-21 in May 1916, one of three such raids in which nine people were killed and twenty-eight badly injured.

### Lady Peckett's Yard

Connects Fossgate with **Pavement** and is named after the wife of John Peckett, a **Lord Mayor of York**. It was called Bacusgail (Bake House Lane) in 1312 and later housed an auctioneers and Richardson's, a money lender. In 1857 **Joseph Rowntree II** rented a building in the yard for one of his many Adult schools where they taught men to read and write, using scripture lessons; women followed soon after. Mary Kitching was president of the 'B' class of Lady Peckett's Yard Ladies School for fourteen years until in 1892 she left to do missionary work in the Holy Land. A lion from a circus in **Parliament Street** escaped and was eventually cornered here in the early 1900s. Nearby in Black Horse Passage Joseph Rowntree set up a soup kitchen in 1845.

Leetham's flour mill from Garden
Place, Hungate in 1904.

## Lady Well

Designed by **John Carr** this is on the **New Walk**; it is variously known as the Pikeing
or Pickering Well. Its waters were reputed to be effective in disorders of the eyes. The
original 1749 brief was 'to contract with proper workmen for making a hansoom
fountain at the pikeing well'. This part of the New Walk was called Pye Kell at the
time.

## Leeman, George

George Leeman (1809-1882) was a lawyer and Liberal MP twice for the City of York.
In 1849 he was chairman of the York, Newcastle and Berwick Railway, succeeding the
'Railway King' **George Hudson** after he helped uncover Hudson's illegal share dealing.
Leeman was deputy chairman of North Eastern Railways from 1855-74 and chairman
from 1874-80. He was **Lord Mayor** three times.

## Leetham's Mill Warehouse

At Hungate, this was one of the largest flour mills in Europe designed by Walter Penty
in 1895 and comprising five storeys and a nine storey water tower complete with
battlements and turrets. It is surrounded on three sides by the **Foss** and Wormald's
Cut. By 1911 more than 600 people worked here. Spillers took it over in 1930 before
removing to Hull in 1931 after a fire; **Rowntrees** bought it in 1937 for cocoa bean
storage.

Lendal Bridge.

## Lendal Bridge

Necessitated by the need for access to the new railway, Lendal Bridge was opened in 1863 to replace the ferry which plied between the Lendal and Barker Towers. Jon Leeman was the last ferryman – he received £15 and a horse and cart in redundancy compensation. The arrival of the railways had exerted considerable pressure on the ferry service and after considerable argument between the Corporation of York and the railway companies the York Improvement Act was passed in 1860 to allow construction of the first Lendal Bridge. It was designed by the aptly-named William Dredge. Unfortunately, this bridge collapsed during construction killing five men; it was replaced by the present bridge, designed by Thomas Page who was responsible also for Skeldergate Bridge here and Westminster Bridge. Lendal Bridge displays the resplendent V&A insignia (honouring Queen Victoria and Prince Albert) and the crossed keys of St Peter symbolizing the **Minster**, with the **Guildhall** in the background. The remnants of Dredge's bridge were dredged up from the river and sold to Scarborough Council who used the remnants in the construction of Valley Bridge.

## Lendal Tower

In 1677 the tower was leased for 500 years to the York Waterworks Company for two peppercorns (a peppercorn rent) and provided York's water supply until 1836 when the dedicated red brick engine house was built. The tower was put on the market for £650,000 in 2001 and sold as a private residence. The peppercorn rent is payable annually until 2177.

Lawrence Street in 1901; a branch of the local Conservative Party about to set off from outside the Tam O' Shanter, destined for Buttercrambe Woods.

## Leper Hospitals

York had at least four mediaeval leper hospitals, or lazar-houses; in the 1990s York Archaeological trust rediscovered the site of the 1108 Augustinian leper hospital of St Nicholas in Lawrence Street; excavations uncovered an aisled hall. St Mary Magdalene was at the end of **Bootham** just past the Burton Stone; another was near Monkbridge, called St Leonard or St Loy. **St Katherine** was outside the city beyond **Micklegate**.

## The 'Little Admiral'

The admiral – perhaps enjoying a promotion – stands on the 1778 clock with his sextant in Coney Street, fixing his position by the sun. He was bombed to the ground during the 1942 **Baedecker Raid** but luckily was found by Eric Milner White, Dean of York, and kept until the restoration of the clock in 1966. A later gas-lit clock was made by Thomas Cooke in 1856. A further restoration was completed in early 2013.

## Little Ease

A tiny prison cell in **Monk Bar** little over 5 feet in diameter. In 1594 Alice Bowman, a local recusant, was held here. From 1845 to 1913 a police inspector lived there, and in other rooms. It is now part of the **Richard III** Museum in the Bar.

## Lord Mayor & Lady Mayoress

Today the Lord Mayor is Chairman of City of York Council and York's first citizen; he is second only to the Lord Mayor of London in precedence; the Sheriff holds the oldest office of Sheriff in England and Wales. The Lord Mayor (in common only with

The inauguration of the Lord Mayor as re-enacted during the 1971 pageant.

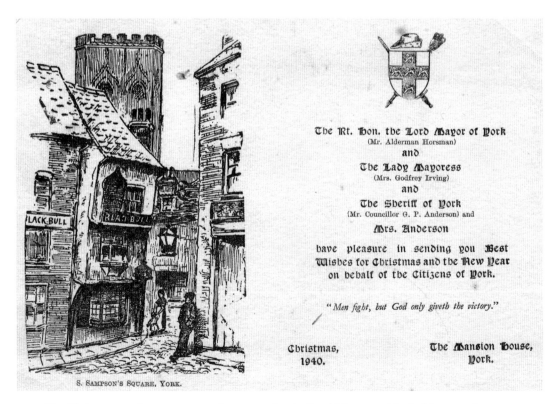

The Christmas card sent out to serving troops by the Lord Mayor and Lady Mayoress in 1940.

Edinburgh and London) carries the title The Right Hon. The Lord Mayor of York. On civic occasions the Lord Mayor is preceded by the civic sword, the silver mace and the Cap of Maintenance; his chains of office are those bequeathed to the office by Sir Robert Watter in 1612. The Cap, also known as the Swordbearer's Hat, is worn by the official bearing the sword and may not be removed during ceremonies, even in church. The Mayor's brief is 'to keep and guard the city for our Lord the King ... to maintain and advance the city's rights and jurisdictions ... and to do right by rich and poor'. According to ancient rule the mayor's wife was, before 1823, officially addressed as Lady: 'he is Lord for a year and a day, but she is Lady for ever and aye'. The Lady Mayoress wears a gold chain presented by Marmaduke Rawdon, **Merchant Adventurer**, in 1665. Hugh de Selby was the city's first Lord Mayor in 1217; Selby exported wool and imported wine; he held the post a further five times, his son John seven times and his grandson Nicholas four times. 800 or so years later the Mayor for 2012-13 is Keith Hyman and Lady Mayoress is Karen Hyman.

## The Lunatic Asylum

Built to **John Carr's** design, it opened in 1777 in **Bootham** with fifteen patients rising to 199 by 1813; its mission was to be caring 'without undue severity'. Part of the asylum burnt down in 1814 with the tragic loss of four patients, and patient records; somewhat convenient, perhaps, as the fire coincided with allegations aimed at the management of the asylum, and with the rise of the **Retreat**, a very different type of psychiatric hospital. All staff were dismissed and replaced. In the same year a visiting magistrate had reported that the 'house is yet in a shocking state ... a number of secret cells in a state of filth horrible beyond description' and the floor covered 'with straw perfectly soaked with urine and excrement'. The asylum advertised that, 'patients are admitted according to their circumstances, the terms for pauper patients belonging to the City, Ainsty and County are 8 shillings per week'. In 1904 it was renamed **Bootham Park Hospital.** In 1777, it was only the fifth purpose built asylum in the country. One of the founders was Dr Alexander Hunter, the hospital's only physician for many years. His publications include *The Medical History of Worms*.

## Mad Alice Lane

Between Swinegate and Low Petergate, it is named after Alice Smith, a resident hanged for the crime of insanity in 1825. It also goes by the less vivid name of Lund's Court.

## Mansion House

Built on the site of the chapel and kitchens of St Christopher's Hall. Mansion House is the official residence of the Right Honourable the **Lord Mayor of York** during his or her year in office. York had a house for its Lord Mayor even before London's Mansion house. York's Mansion House is based on the Queen's Gallery at Somerset House in London which was designed by Inigo Jones and built between 1723 and 1733 on the site of the chapel of the Guild of St Christopher. It houses the York Civic Plate and Insignia – notably the sword of the Emperor Sigismund which originally hung over his stall as Knight of the Garter in St George's Chapel, Windsor and given to York in

Mansion House in about 1800, from a watercolour by Thomas White.

1439. Sigismund was King of Hungary and Croatia from 1387 to 1437, and Holy Roman Emperor from 1433-1437. The Mansion House is famously threatened with being burnt to the ground in Gaskell's *Sylvia's Lovers* (1863) if the Mayor, in 1777, failed to satisfy the demands of the **press-gang**. The architect remains a mystery; it may have been **William Etty**. Doncaster has the only other Mansion House outside York and London.

## Mapping York

The brainchild of Dr Peter Addyman, chairman of York Civic Trust, whose idea it was to create a cartographic study of the city's development soon after he founded York Archaeological Trust in 1972. The forty-year project to map York's history will soon be finished: it comprises a series of maps showing how the city developed from Roman times to the present day and will be complemented with essays by leading academics. The project is part of a European initiative launched in 1955 to create a library of maps for historic cities across the continent. Its basis was an Ordnance Survey map of York from 1852 which details the streets and buildings of the city from AD71 and in the Anglo-Saxon, medieval and Victorian periods.

# WHEREAS
# JONATHAN MARTIN

Stands Charged with having on the Night of the 1st of February, Instant,

## WILFULLY SET FIRE TO

# *YORK* MINSTER.

## A REWARD OF
# 100 *POUNDS*

## Will be Paid on his being Apprehended and Lodged in any of his Majesty's Gaols.

### *And a Further Reward of*

# One Hundred Pounds

Will be paid on the Conviction of any ACCOMPLICES of the said JONATHAN MARTIN, to such Person or Persons as shall give Information which may lead to such Conviction.

*The following is a Description of the said Jonathan Martin: viz.*

He is rather a Stout Man, about Five Feet Six Inches high, with light Hair cut close, coming to a point in the centre of the Forehead, and high above the Temples, and has large bushy Red Whiskers; he is between Forty and Fifty Years of Age, and of singular Manners. He usually wears a single-breasted blue Coat, with a stand-up Collar, and Buttons covered with the same cloth; a black cloth Waistcoat; and blue cloth Trowsers; Half-Boots laced-up in front; and a glazed, broad-brimmed, low-crowned Hat. Sometimes he wears a double-breasted blue Coat with yellow Buttons.—When Travelling, he wears a large black leather Cape coming down to his Elbows, with two Pockets within the Cape; there is a square piece of dark coloured Fur, extending from one shoulder point to the other.—At other times he wears a drab coloured great Coat, with a large Cape and shortish Skirts—When seen at York last Sunday, he had on the double-breasted blue Coat, a common Hat, and his great Coat.

The said JONATHAN MARTIN is a Hawker of a Pamphlet entitled "The Life of Jonathan Martin, of Darlington, Tanner," the Third Edition of which is printed at Lincoln, by R. E. LEARY, 1828.—He had lodged in York about a Month, and quitted it on the 27th of January last, stating that he was going to Tadcaster for a few Days, and thence to Leeds. He returned to York on the 31st of January, and said that he and his Wife had taken Lodgings in Leeds. He was not seen in York after the 1st of February.

*By Order of the DEAN and CHAPTER of YORK,*
## CHRIST. JNO. NEWSTEAD,
*Clerk of the Peace for the Liberty of St. Peter of York.*

*York, 5th February,* 1829.

BARNES & CO. PRINTERS, NORTH SHIELDS.

## Margaret Tudor, Queen Dowager of Scotland

Visited York in 1503 and again in 1516 and 1517 on her way to and from a visit to her brother, Henry VIII. She stayed at **St Mary's Abbey** on both occasions. In 1503 she was met by two Sheriffs of York and 100 citizens on horseback, along with the city's great and good. At **Micklegate Bar** the **Mayor**, Recorder and Alderman met her in their finery. **Queen Margaret's Arch** is named after her but was built for her father, Henry VII.

## Martin, Jonathan

Minster arsonist who on 1 February 1829 started the first **Minster fire**. Plagued by depression he had previous form for threatening to murder the Bishop of Oxford and was committed to West Auckland Lunatic Asylum. Some years later and living in York, Martin was irritated by a buzzing coming from the organ while attending Evensong. He hid in the bell tower until the doors were locked and shinned down a bell rope to the nave where he piled hymn and prayer books into two bonfires and set them alight. He stole a Bible 'on the Lord's orders' and made his escape. The organ and choir were amongst the fixtures and fittings destroyed. Martin was arrested and tried at York **Castle**; the jury found him guilty but the judge overruled and declared him not guilty on the grounds of insanity. He was committed to the Criminal Lunatic Asylum in London, where he died on 27 May 1838. One good result of Martin's action was the re-establishment of the **Minster Police** and the employment of a fire watchman cum constable.

## Marygate Landing

The **River Ouse** was crucial to York from earliest times, right through the **Roman** and **Viking** occupations and the Middle Ages, making York an important port. Evidence of Irish and German boats date from around 1125. Some **Stonegate** buildings are said to be built with ships' timbers; there is also a fine figurehead in the same street.

## Maundy

The first known Royal Maundy took place in Knaresborough in 1210, during a visit by King John. Records (mainly in *Rotulus Misae*) show that on 5 April 1210, the *Die Jovis Cene* (on the Day of the Lord's Supper) King John, staying at Knaresborough Castle, gave to thirteen poor men of Knaresborough, Maundy gifts of thirteen pennies each, a robe, breeches, a girdle, a knife and shoes. The figure of thirteen was a reference to the numbers of diners at the Last Supper, not to the monarch's reign or age, as in later tradition where a red purse of money is given 'in lieu of clothing'. Following Maundy Thursday, King John observed Good Friday by providing a meal in Knaresborough for a hundred paupers (costing 9s 4½d) and a thousand more in Yorkshire (£4 13s 9d), both meals including bread and fish. The Queen distributed Maundy Money in York in 1972; she visited York again during her Diamond Jubilee Year on Maundy Thursday, 5 April 2012, a fitting adjunct to the York 800 celebrations marking the 800th anniversary of the signing of the city's charter.

## Medical & Surgical School

The present Hull-York Medical School is York's second medical school. The first was founded in 1834, spurred on by members of **York Medical Society**. Unfortunately, it was short lived and closed in 1858, but not before it had attracted renowned teachers like George Stubbs (anatomy and later painter); **John Burton** (obstetrician and **Laurence Sterne's** Dr Slop); John Hughlings Jackson (d. 1911), neurologist and house physician to the **York Dispensary** – the new medical school building bears his name; Daniel Hack Tuke (d. 1895, great grandson of **William Tuke**), psychiatrist who trained at the **Retreat**; James Atkinson (d. 1839), surgeon, friend of Sterne and author of *Medical Bibliography*; the dedication reads : 'To all idle medical students in Great Britain'.

## Memorial Gardens

The main feature of this pleasant space which opened in 1925 is the War Memorial designed by Sir Edward Lutyens who was also responsible for The Cenotaph in Whitehall. The annual Service of Remembrance is held here; there is a special memorial to the Korean War fallen. Other York memorials are in **Rowntree Park**, set up in 1921 for **Rowntree** employees, with a set of listed gates added to remember those who died in the Second World War; Duncombe Place and Skeldergate Island (Green Howards) – both Boer War memorials; and Acomb Green – the First and Second World Wars. The **NER** memorial in Station Road remembers the 2,236 employees who died in the first war.

## Merchant Adventurer's Hall

In Fossgate, this fine building was built on the site of the original 1357 building in 1667; the fifteenth-century Great Hall and Chapel of Holy Trinity still survive, as do Mercer's records going back to the early fourteenth century. These provide us with a wealth of information on **trade** in York at the time. The Hall is one of York's four surviving guildhalls for the fifty or so mercantile and craft guilds here; the others are the **Guildhall, Merchant Taylor's** in Aldwark, and **St Anthony's Hall** in Peaseholme Green. Typically for guildhalls it had two mutual functions: the secular trade side, and the religious guild (originally The Fraternal and Guild of Our Lord and the Blessed Virgin, assuming its current name in 1581) to which commercial profits were channelled to justify the business activity and to finance the hospital which was in the Undercroft. The French motto is 'God give us good (business) ventures'. It was made about 1850 by M. N. Hassey, who also carved the bust of Shakespeare at the **York Theatre Royal** and a statue of the Virgin Mary at the **Bar Convent**. The Company used the coat of arms of the Merchant Adventurers of England until 1969 when they were granted their own. The lower part of the Hall is built mainly of brick – the earliest surviving made in York after the **Romans**.

## Meynell, Alicia

The first woman jockey to compete in a horse race against men, at the **Knavesmire** in 1755 when she rode Vingarella side-saddle. Victory, though, had to wait until the following year when she won on Louisa, again at the Knavesmire.

## Micklegate Bar

Micklegate Bar was originally called Mickleith which means great gate; the royal arms are those of Edward III; the arch is Norman, the rest fourteenth century, the side arch was added in 1753. Being on the road to and from London this was the Bar through which royal visitors entered York. Edward IV, **Richard III**, Henry VII, Margaret Tudor, James I, Charles I (on three Civil War occasions) and James II all passed through. Henry VIII was scheduled to enter here but, in the event, came in through **Walmgate Bar.** Heads and quarters of traitors were routinely displayed on the top, most famously: Lord **Scrope** of Mastan in 1415; Sir Henry Percy (Hotspur) after his part in the rebellion against Elizabeth I; Richard Duke of York after the Battle of Wakefield in 1460, prompting Shakespeare to write: 'Off with his head and set it on York's gates; so York did overlook the town of York' (Queen Margaret in *Henry VI); Thomas Percy in 1569 – his head remained there for two years. Removal of heads without permission was, not inappropriately, punishable by beheading – guess where the heads ended up? The last displays were in 1746 after the Jacobite Rebellion at Culloden. The heads of James Mayne and William Connelly remained on the Bar until 1754. The barbican was removed in 1826 to allow a circus access to the city; the east side arch was built in 1827.

## Micklegate Hill

Required a three horse hand for the horse-drawn trams: a trace horse being held in reserve to provide additional horse power should one of the other two not make it.

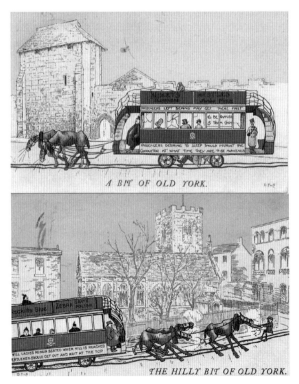

*A BIT OF OLD YORK.*

*THE HILLY BIT OF OLD YORK.*

*Left:* Two of the postcards published to highlight the cruelty shown to horses in York.

*Opposite:* The Minster.

A horse by the name of Dobbin reputedly did the job for many years making his own way back down the hill to his post outside the post office until next required. Accusations of cruelty towards the horses led to the publication of a series of comic postcards mocking the York Tramway Company.

## Military Sunday
Set up in 1885 by the then Dean, the Very Reverend Purey Cust, as a memorial to General Gordon killed in Khartoum in 1884. The Sundays lasted until 1939 and were hugely popular with some people walking through the night to attend them.

## The Minster
The official name is The Cathedral and Metropolitical Church of St Peter in York. It is the largest mediaeval building in England and the biggest cathedral in Europe north of the Alps. It towers on the site of an earlier Norman cathedral which was almost as huge and

York from Clifford's Tower.

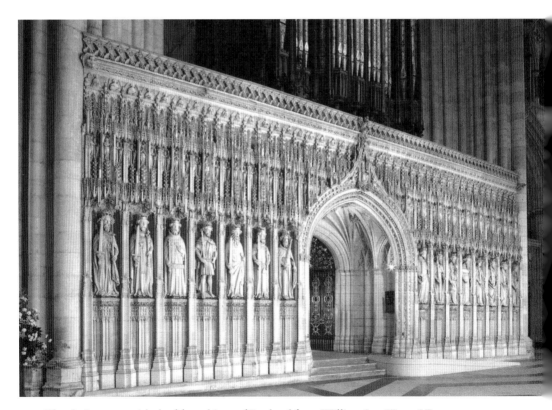

The choir screen with the fifteen kings of England from William I to Henry VI.

Postcard published celebrating Jonathan Martin's trial and conviction and the specially produced tea pot souvenir.

took 250 years to build from 1220 to 1470. Its treasures are countless. They include 128 stained glass windows from the twelfth to the twenty-first century, most notable of which is the 1408 Great East Window – the size of a tennis court – the world's largest area of stained glass. The Minster is built in the shape of a cross, facing east towards Jerusalem.

### Minster Fires

They say all things come in threes: devastating fires at York **Minster** are no exception. The first was in 1829 when the arsonist **Jonathan Martin** destroyed the archbishop's throne, the pulpit and the choir; after this the Dean and Chapter resolved to reinstate the lapsed post of night watchman. The second followed in 1840 when clockmaker William Groves left a candle burning and caused the south west tower to go up in flames. The York Operative Protestants Association were in session nearby and declared it a Catholic hoax. After this the Dean and Chapter, wincing no doubt at the combined £105,560 repair bills, resolved to insure the Minster. The last was in 1984: UFOs and divine retribution were ruled out and an improvident lightning strike given as the most likely cause. Whatever, the South Transept roof was destroyed and the Rose window shattered. Four years later the painstaking repairs were completed, including bosses in the South Transept vaulting designed by winners of a *Blue Peter* competition. Johnathan Martin's fire burnt all night and was only discovered next morning when a boy called Swinbank skated by and fell over, only to see smoke pouring out of a nave window. City fire engines eventually arrived but the firemen were 'old and incapacitated … of little use'. It took until evening and eight further engines to control the fire: the Yorkshire Insurance engine, one from the Cavalry Barracks, Beilby Thompson's from Escrick, four from Leeds and one from Tadcaster.

Minster Library and the sadly demolished Deanery in 1952.

The first Deanery, demolished in 1831.

## The Minster Library

The Old Palace not only houses **York Minster's** library and archives but also the Collections Department and the conservation studio. It is known as The Old Palace because part of the building used to be the chapel of the thirteenth-century Archbishop's palace. In 1810 it was refurbished and, shortly after, the Minster's collection was installed there. The original library was the dream and ambition of King Egbert, a disciple of the Venerable Bede: he opened a school of international repute and started a collection of books. The librarianship then passed from 778-781 to Flaccus Albinus Alcuinus, better known as **Alcuin**. He later become one of the architects of the Carolingian Renaissance. Alcuin's catalogue featured works by many of the Church Fathers and classical authors such as Pliny, Aristotle, Cicero and Virgil – but all was tragically lost when the Minster and library were sacked by the Vikings. It was not until the eighteenth century that the collection started to grow significantly: from 1716 to 1820, there were more than 1,200 loans by 179 different borrowers. **Laurence Sterne,** author of *The Life and Opinions of Tristram Shandy, Gentleman* was a regular user. By 1810 there were nearly 8,000 volumes and the library moved to its present home in Dean's Park ; in 1890 Edward Hailstone bequeathed 10,000 volumes. Sadly, many books were sold to raise money for repairs, including a 1519 Erasmus' *New Testament* for £20,000; however, the proceeds went to the new Library Fund started in 1945; today it is unquestionably the finest cathedral library in Britain .

## Minster Policeman

Grew out of the office of Constable of the Liberty . In 1285 the Minster Close was enclosed by a 12-foot-high wall within which the Dean and Chapter held sway and, until 1839 had a Liberty of their own – the Liberty of Saint Peter and Peter Prison which, in turn, had its own Chief Constable, constables, coroners, magistrates, bailiffs, stewards and under-stewards. After the **Jonathan Martin** fire of 1829 the Dean and Chapter decreed that 'Henceforward a watchman/constable shall be employed to keep watch every night in and about the cathedral'. Minster Police antedate the establishment of Sir Robert Peel's police force; indeed, Peel will have be influenced by the Minster Police when he visited his sister who was married to the then Dean, William Cockburn. York **Minster** is one of seven cathedrals in the world which have their own constabulary or police force. The others are Liverpool's Anglican Cathedral; Canterbury, Hereford and Chester Cathedrals; St Peter's Basilica in Rome (the Swiss Guard) and Washington's National Cathedral . The phrase 'taking a liberty' stems from the police here when in the thirteenth century the **Lord Mayor** persisted in entering the Liberty of St Peter to harass the residents. The Pope intervened to stop him 'taking a liberty'. Today the job of the Minster Police is mainly security, fire watching and looking after the 380 or so sets of keys.

## The Minster School

Formerly known as the Minster Song School; **Alcuin** (c. AD 732-804) was a master here. It specialises in music and singing: of the 180 or so pupils, forty are choristers at York **Minster**. In addition to singing the early choristers had to read lessons, carry the cross

Not many football pitches can boast a backdrop like this; originally published in John Roden's *The Minster School, York: A Centenary History 1903-2004.*

Two old old boys, courtesy of John Roden.

and candles in procession, swing censers, see to the numerous changes of cope for the celebrant during the mass and hold the *Book* for the gospeller. There were three rows of seats, or forms – giving us the derivation of 'forms', as in school desk. In 1903 Dean Purey-Cust made arrangements for a vacant building in Minster Yard to be used as the new song school. Before Deangate was closed to traffic in 1989 pupils were obliged to doff their caps at motorists who allowed them to cross the road en route to the Minster.

## Mistletoe at the Minster

York **Minster** is the only cathedral in the county which adorns its altar with holly *and* mistletoe at Christmas, despite its Druidic connections and the traditional ban on its display in churches. At York it traditionally formed part of a service of repentance where transgressors could seek forgiveness. The priest would hold out a branch and say: 'public and universal liberty, pardon and freedom of all sorts of inferior wicked people at the Minster gates and the gates of the city, towards the four quarters of heaven'.

## Monk Bar

Built around 1330 it was originally called Monkgate Bar; at 63 feet it is the tallest of York's Bars. Designed as a self-contained fortress, assailants had to cross each floor to reach the next flight of stairs, thus exposing themselves to defensive fire. A perfect fortress, the Bar features loopholes (for bows and arrows); gun ports and murder holes from which heavy objects and boiling water might be dropped. The coat of arms is Plantagenet. The Bar was used as a prison in the sixteenth century for recusant Catholics, and others: in 1588 Robert Walls was imprisoned for 'drawing blood in a fray'. The barbican was removed in the early 1800s. To rent the rooms at the top, one Thomas Pak (Master Mason at the **Minster**) paid 4*s* per annum.

## Morrell, John Bowes (1873-1963)

As with **William Etty** and **WA Evelyn** we have much to thank JB Morrell for when it comes to saving York and its buildings from mindless destruction. Invaluable work for York Conservation Trust (which he co-founded) apart, Morell was a director at **Rowntrees** from age twenty-five, **Lord Mayor** twice (in 1914 and 1950) and a powerful voice in the establishment of the **University of York**. The library there is named after him.

## Mother Shipton

Born in 1488 (so predating Nostradamus by fifteen years) in a cave next to the River Nidd, the legendary Mother Shipton (nee Ursula Southeil) is synonymous with the art of prophecy. Afflicted by what was probably scoliosis and variously branded a witch and the devil's daughter her predictions have included the demise of Cardinal Wolsey, the Gunpowder Plot, the Great Fire of London, her own death , and, as yet inaccurately, the end of the world (1881 and 1991). The earliest mention of her did not appear until 1641. This describes how, when living in York, she had predicted that the out of favour Cardinal Wolsey, who planned to be enthroned as **Archbishop** in 1530, would see York, but never reach the city. Wolsey got as far as Cawood Castle, and from the tower saw

**York Minster** in the distance, vowing he would have Mother Shipton burnt as a witch. But he was arrested on a charge of high treason, and died on the journey south. This first printed version of the (post-eventum) prophecies spread the fame of Mother Shipton throughout England. Ursula married Thomas Shipton of Shipton-by-Beningborough.

## The Mount School

The story of The Mount School begins with Esther Tuke, second wife of **William Tuke**, who in 1785 opened the boarding school in Trinity Lane, off Micklegate and known then as the Friends' Girl School. The aims of the York school were heavily influenced by the famous Quaker school at Ackworth near Pontefract, founded in 1779 by John Fothergill and which, in turn, was previously a (particularly insalubrious) branch of the London Foundling Hospital in Bloomsbury. Fothergill, a Quaker physician, teamed up with William Tuke and David Barclay (of banking fame) to open the school for Quaker children 'not of affluence'; despite best intentions it had a reputation for being 'harsh, if not barbarous'. Pupils included the daughters of Abraham Darby III of Coalbrookdale, the famous ironmaker. In 1796 purpose-built premises were bought for £450 in Tower Street near to **York Castle** and the Friends' Meeting House. William Tuke retired in 1804 with the school in financial difficulties; it closed in 1812. In 1829 Samuel Tuke established the York Friends' Boys' School (later **Bootham School**) and then turned his attentions to establishing a girls' equivalent along the same lines. This materialised in Castlegate House in 1831, the 1763 mansion of the Recorder of York. Girls attended the lectures given by the **Yorkshire Philosophical Society**, adding to and annotating their own collections of shells, minerals and pressed plants. In 1855 the lease on Castlegate expired, thus triggering the move to the purpose-built buildings at the Mount under the supervision of Rachel Tregelles. Lydia Rous took over as superintendent in 1866 and it was she who ensured that Mount girls entered the new public examinations. The University of London was not interested; to them 'girls were poorly educated and therefore incapable of taking a degree course' but Cambridge University, which established Emily Davies' Girton College for women in 1873, took them on board. Alumni include actors Mary Ure and Dame Judi Dench; the three Drabble sisters: writers A. S. Byatt and Margaret, and art historian Helen Langdon; astronomer Jocelyn Bell Burnell; and TV correspondent Kathy Killick.

## The Mount Junior School

In 1901, under the aegis of Winifred Sturge, a graduate of London University's Westfield College, the Mount Junior School opened, founded on Montessori principles and included amongst its former pupils the Marxist historian Christopher Hill, six of the children of Arnold and Mary Rowntree and William Sessions, the York printer and publisher, and his sister.

## Mucky Peg Lane

Off St Sampson's Square, now Finkle Street, the lane was a notorious haunt for prostitutes – which presumably accounts for the name. An alternative etymology derives from Mucky Pig Lane.

## Multangular Tower

This ten sided tower is in **Museum Gardens**; the lower 20 feet are Roman, from around 310 and constitute the only such surviving tower in Britain. It formed the western extremity of the fortress and features a stone 21 feet by 11 feet wide, bearing the legible inscription '*Genio loci feliciter*' – 'good luck to the guardian spirit of this place'. Its name originates in 1683, before that it was called Ellerendyng or Elrondyng. A fountain stood near here in a pool from 1838; the fountain disappeared in 1917 and was found in 1967 in a garden in Manor Drive, Acomb. It is now in Fairfax House. Another multangular tower apparently stood in Feasegate.

## Museum Gardens

The gardens were designed in the 'Gardenesque' style by landscape architect, Sir John Murray Naysmith in the 1830s in 4 acres formerly known as Manor Shore. They show off the buildings of the Museum and Abbey at their best while also providing space for displaying plant specimens as a Botanical Garden. As more and more exotic specimens were introduced, a conservatory was built to house tropical plants such as sugar cane, coffee, tea, ginger and cotton as well as orchids and epiphytes. A pond was created to accommodate a large rare water-lily, the *Victoria amazonica*. Although

Museum Gardens from Lendal Bridge in the 1930s.

The Boat Yard at Manor Shore, from a wood engraving originally published in *Eighty Three Views in York* printed by John Hill, Marygate 1838.

the pond and the conservatory are long gone, the 10-acre gardens are still a listed Botanical Garden and contain many varieties of trees, deciduous and evergreen, native and exotic. From 1835 until 1961 an entrance fee was charged. York Swimming Bath Company's pool opened in 1837; it was closed in 1922 and filled in, during 1969.

### Mutton Curry, Hangman

In 1802 William Curry (or Curry Wilkinson, or Thomas Askern) was sentenced to death for sheep stealing (for which he earned the nickname Mutton Curry) and was destined for the long drop at the **Knavesmire**. Fortunately, though, a hangman was needed at the Castle and Curry was offered the job. By 1810 he had performed twenty-five **executions**, including a number of convicted Luddites from Cartwright's Mill at Rawfolds, as described in Charlotte Bronte's 1849 *Shirley*. All did not always go well though. In 1821 he reported to the scaffold somewhat drunk and unable to find the doomed William Brown's neck; he was beaten up on his way home for his ineptitude; later that year he was about to hang five prisoners when he, again worse the wear for drink, fell down the drop with the convicts. He retired, twenty hangings later, *otium sine dignitate* to the Thirsk Poor House in 1835. *The Yorkshire Gazette* pointed out that 'gin was apt to provide a snare for him'.

### The Mystery Plays

The Mystery Plays were revived during the 1951 York Festival of the Arts; they were performed on a fixed stage in the **Museum Gardens** – it was not until 1954 that a wagon

The cover of the 1969 *Mystery Pays & Festival of Arts* programme.

play, *The Flood*, toured the streets. The 1951 production was the most popular Festival of Britain event in the country, with over 26,000 people seeing the plays. The word 'mystery' in this context means a 'trade' or 'craft' in mediaeval English; it is also, of course, a religious truth or rite. The mediaeval plays were traditionally sponsored by the city's craft guilds. Nowadays, the mediaeval *Corpus Christi* plays are produced every four years, most recently in 2012, by the York Guilds and Companies. Hitherto the *Creation* to the *Last Judgement* is paraded through the streets on pageant wagons as actors perform selections from the forty-eight high points of Christian history at twelve playing stations designated by the city banners with one guild taking responsibility for one episode. The sole surviving manuscript of the York plays, from around 1465, is in the British Library.

### Napoleon Bonaparte
Napoleon arrived in York in 1822, one year after his death on St Helena. He stood sentinel outside a tobacconists in Low Ousegate, H. Clarke, to whom letters were addressed simply as 'Napoleon, York' – and would arrive. In full uniform, he is proffering a snuffbox to passers-by; he is carved out of a solid piece of oak and was one of three made, selling for £50.00 each. Apparently he frequently ended up in the **River Ouse**, courtesy of soldiers garrisoned in York.

*'Du tabac à priser, monsieur?'*

### Narrow Lop Lane
Or Little Blake Street accessed through Peter Gate and widened in 1860 and 1864 to form **Duncombe Place** and a vista of the Minster. Etridge's Royal Hotel, a coaching inn, was in Blake Street, demolished in 1859 for the York Poor Law Union.

### The National Railway Museum
It was the Science Museum in London – known then as the Patent Office Museum – which started the country's collection of railway artefacts when they purchased *Rocket* in 1866. The North Eastern Railway then opened a public railway museum in Queen's Street, York in 1927. In the 1930s, all the other railway companies had their own railway related collections which were all combined in 1948 after nationalisation. In 1975 the National Railway Museum opened in Leeman Road. The 8ft 10in diameter railway wheels outside are probably the largest locomotive wheels in existence; they were cast at Bristol in 1873 to drive 4-2-4 Tender Loco No 40, an express passenger train of the Bristol & Exeter Railway.

### Needham, John Peacock
A Lendal surgeon heavily preoccupied with the first cholera epidemic. When it ended in 1833 Needham worked hard to discover more about the disease and published his *Facts & Observations Related to the Disease Commonly Called Cholera as it has Recently Prevailed in the City of York*.

## Nestle Archive

A new Nestlé UK state of the art archive at the Haxby Road site was launched in 2011. Many of the items, which include 37,000 photographs and over 100 hours of film, are being exhibited at various places and at various events in the city on an ongoing basis.

## The New Drop

In 1868 the New Drop replaced the public gallows which had moved from the **Knavesmire** in 1801; it was situated where the roundabout at St George's car park is today. Roughly opposite in the **Castle Museum** wall is a small doorway through which the condemned were led to the gallows. The last public **execution** was of Frederick Parker in 1868, a convicted murderer: 5,000 people came to watch. After that hangings were behind closed doors at the New Drop. The last man to hang in York under the black flag was August Carlsen who was hanged at the New Drop on 29 February 1896 for the murder of Julia Wood.

## New Earswick

The objective of the Joseph Rowntree Trust when it developed the idea of the new garden village was to provide even the worker with the lowest means a new type of house that was clean, sanitary and efficient. **Rowntree's** deep concern for the welfare of his workers, the research findings of his son, **Seebohm**, into the plight of the urban poor, his Quaker beliefs and the pioneering work on garden cities by **Ebenezer Howard** all combined to drive the establishment of New Earswick. The Folk Hall is the nucleus of the village; it was built in 1907 at a cost of £2,278 15s 1½d. Rowntree actively encouraged women to get out of the home and to use the many facilities offered there: 'In this country it seems to be the thought that women do not need recreation' he pondered, citing the example of Germany where it was, and still is, the norm for families to go out together as families, with the children. During the First World War the hall was used to offer hospitality to Belgian refugees. The village library was here from 1908 with the first 100 books donated by Joseph Rowntree. One of the main functions of the Hall was as a place of worship – for all faiths. However, over time, a Wesleyan Chapel and a place for Anglican worship were established while the Society of Friends and Roman Catholics continued to use the Hall. From 1945 it was home to the village nursery until its move to the **primary school** in 1997.

## New Earswick Primary School

The first 'school' was in the Folk Hall set up in 1909 for twenty-five infants. The permanent school was built 1912 for 352 five to fourteen year olds to save them the trek to Haxby Road; the school, the 'Open Air School', was a model of enlightenment: boys and girls were taught the same subjects (science teaching was usually the preserve of boys) and all the windows faced south, opened to an extent of 18 feet and were at head level to maximise natural daylight. Each child had 15 square feet of floor area – 50 per cent more than was required by the Board of Education then. The fine clock on the cupola was donated by Joseph Stephenson Rowntree. The opening ceremony, attended by local dignitaries led by **Joseph Rowntree**, attracted a number of suffragettes

GREETINGS
— from —
NEW
EARSWICK

who threw bricks through the windows; Miss Violet Key Jones jumped on the running board of Sir Walter Worsley's car and went on to the Folk Hall to scatter pamphlets urging 'Votes for Women.'

## The New Walk

The place to promenade in the eighteenth century, it was laid down in 1730, with its sixty-four elms and sixty-six limes trees planted in 1732, although records exist of a walk here from 1547. In 1739 it was extended beyond the Blue Bridge with a further 340 elms. All of the trees were replaced by 820 new ones in 1824. A succession of bridges spanned the Ouse here, the fourth of which was flanked by two Russian cannon presented to the city in 1858 after the 1855 Siege of Sebastopol. They were sold for scrap in 1941 as part of the war effort. The newest bridge is the elegant Millennium Bridge, inspired by the spokes of a bicycle. The present Blue Bridge, the latest of five – all blue – was built in 1930 on the site of the original 1730 wooden blue bridge. In 1754 the **York Courant** declared that the New Walk was 'one of the most agreeable publick walks in the Kingdom for its great neatness, beautiful town and situation seen in its prospect ... not unlike nor inferior to any of the views in Venice'.

## New York

Named after James, eighth **Duke of York** (later James II) after his capture of New Amsterdam in 1664.

The New Walk as in Nathan Drake's *The Noble Terras Walk of York*, 1756.

The New Walk in the 1920s.

### The Norman House
An often overlooked treasure in the yard of 52 **Stonegate**. It is the oldest domestic building in York and was very large, obviously owned by a man of some wealth.

### North Eastern Railway Company Headquarters
The building completed in 1906, now a five star hotel, is a magnificent, if extravagant, testament to the power and wealth of the early railways, indeed a 'huge palace of business'. The striking coat of arms includes heraldic elements from the principal cities of those railways which merged in 1854 to form the NER: York (lions), Leeds (castles), Berwick (bear and oak). Other marvellous features include a gargoyle type figure on the facade and a steam train weather vane.

### The Observatory
The Observatory was completed in 1833; its 4in refractor telescope was built by York's **Thomas Cooke** in 1850 before he went on to make what was then the largest telescope in the world. York played a crucial role in the development of astronomy in the 1780s when two prominent astronomers – the deaf and dumb **John Goodricke** (1764-1786) and Edward Pigott laid the foundations of variable star astronomy – the study of stars of varying brightness. Goodricke has a college at the **University of York** named after him and Pigott was the first Englishman to discover a comet which subsequently took his name. The Observatory also has an 1811 clock which tells the time based on the positions of stars. At one time it was *the* clock by which all others in York were set and is still always four minutes, twenty seconds, behind GMT. In the mid-nineteenth century

you had to be a member of the **Yorkshire Philosophical Society** or it would cost you sixpence to check a timepiece against the Observatory Clock. The York Observatory originated from a promise made at the very first meeting of the **British Association for the Advancement of Science**, which took place under the auspices of the **Yorkshire Philosophical Society** at the **Yorkshire Museum** in 1831. The Vice President of the Royal Astronomical Society, Dr Pearson, promised that if an observatory were built in York he would personally supply two of his best instruments. He duly obliged, also providing other scientific instruments – including the aforementioned clock. The conical roof was designed by John Smeaton, who also created the Eddystone Lighthouse. Today the observatory houses a telescope made by Thomas Cooke in 1850 with which you can see the stars and planets at night and safely observe the Sun during the day.

## The Odeon

Opened in 1937 in Blossom Street on the site of the Crescent Cafe & Dance Salon typical of Oscar Deutsch's Art Deco 'palaces for the people'. They were intended to evoke luxury liners and to exude luxury in contrast to the ordinariness found in most pre-war homes. A Union Flag flew from the roof whenever a British film was showing. Odeon derives from 'Oscar Deutsch Entertains our Nation?' Not a bit of it: the odeons were named after the ancient Greek for a building used for a musical performance.

## Ye Olde Starre Inne

York's oldest licensed public house, serving us since at least 1644. The striking gallows sign of the Olde Starre Inne still stretches across the street – originally erected in 1733 by landlord Thomas Bulmer who was obliged to pay the owner of the building over the street on to which it joined – 5s rent per year. In 1886 it read '*Boddy's Star Inn*'; the pub is named after Charles I – popularly known as '*the Old Star*' and was used as a Civil War morgue, field station and operating theatre by the Parliamentarians, much to the disgust of the Royalist landlord. The cellar is tenth century and the well was once the only source of clean water in the area.

## Osbaldwick

Osbaldwick is Osbaldeuuic in *Domesday*, derived from Osbald after a Northumbrian earl who ruled here in the eighth century. Osbaldwick borders on the **Roman** road from York (Eboracum) to Brough (Petuaria). A number of erratics (huge glacial deposit boulders of Shap granite) used to lie on the village green which are now in the Yorkshire **Museum Gardens**.

## Our Lady's Row

Goodramgate is named after Guthrum, a Danish chief active around 878. The Grade I listed Lady Row cottages (numbers 60-72) date from 1316. They are the oldest surviving jettied cottages in Britain. Originally nine or ten houses for the priests at neighbouring **Holy Trinity** church, the one at the southern end was demolished in 1766 to make way for a gateway to the thirteenth to fifteenth-century Holy Trinity church. They each comprised one room 10 by 15 feet on each floor. Rents collected went to pay for

Old Ouse Bridge in 1807 – showing St William's Chapel demolished with the bridge in 1809; the tower in the distance belongs to St Martin's in Micklegate.

chantries to the blessed Virgin Mary in nearby churches. Two pubs occupied the cottages at various times: *The Hawk's Crest* from 1796-1819 and *The Noah's Ark* around 1878.

## Ouse Bridge

'The fairest arch in England'. The very first bridge to span the **Ouse** was built by the **Romans** at the end of what is now **Stonegate**; the Vikings replaced this in 850 with their wooden bridge. This collapsed in 1154 under the weight of spectators congregating to see the return of **St William of York** from exile in Sicily after his reinstatement. William made the sign of the cross on seeing the calamity unfold: no one died (one horse suffered a broken leg) and the event was immediately declared a miracle. This bridge was replaced by a stone bridge, part of which was swept away by floods in 1564-5. The new central arch spanned 81 feet; **Defoe**, in his *Tour Through the Whole Island of Great Britain* soberly described it as 'near 70 foot in diameter; it is, without exception, the greatest in England, some say it's as large as the Rialto at Venice, though I think not.' There were about fifty shops, a prison or kidcote, a town hall and a hospital on the bridge and from 1367 England's first public toilets are reputed to have opened here (issuing into the river): 'the place on Owsbridge callyd the pyssing howes'. Agnes Gretehede was paid two shillings a year to keep them clean in 1544. The present Ouse Bridge was built between 1810 and 1821.

## Pageant, The York Historic

The 1909 *Pageant* was a dramatisation of York's history in seven episodes from 800 BC to AD 1644. With a cast of 2,500 the truly epic production involved 800 costume

A page from The Book of York Pageant, 1909.

designs by forty different artists and 2,000 tracings were made and coloured – all based on information supplied by such authorities as the British Museum, Magdalen College, Oxford and Ampleforth College; the chorus comprised 220 singers. *The Mystery Plays* had been bowdlerised (with scenes involving the Virgin Mary cut) and then completely suppressed in 1569; it wasn't until 1909 when this revival of sorts took place, performed in and around the **Museum Gardens**. It included a parade of the banners of the York Guilds through the streets, accompanying a wagon representing the Nativity. Later that year a selection of six plays was performed as a fund-raising venture for St Olave's Church. The *Pageant* was never intended as a religious ceremony although it inevitably included religious episodes: these are inextricably wound up in any 'dramatic representation of the evolution of the old northern capital of Britain'.

### Pavement

Pavement is called thus because around 1329 it was the only clear piece of paved land in the centre of the city. Paving was unusual then. Before that it was called Marketshire and was the site of markets (there once was a market cross here), proclamations and public punishments in days when the punishment was made, and seen, to fit the crime: for example, drunks were made to stand on barrels with pint pots on their heads and goose thieves were put in the stocks with goose wings draped unceremoniously around their necks. Catholic Thomas Percy, Earl of Northumberland, was **executed** here in 1572 for his opposition to Elizabeth I. The Market Cross was demolished in 1813 to make room for more market stalls.

## Peckitt, William

William Peckitt was born in Husthwaite in 1731 – one of England's foremost glass painters and stain glass makers – in fact he is widely regarded as the most prominent and prolific glazier of his day and responsible for keeping the craft alive in the eighteenth century. Patrons included the Dean of York and Horace Walpole with commissions at New College, Oxford and the cathedrals at Exeter, Lincoln and Ripon. The family moved to York around 1750 where William worked in his father's glove making business before setting himself up as a glass painter in Colliergate. He died in 1776 and is buried in **St Martin-cum-Gregory** where Mary, his wife, made a memorial window to him in the church next to a memorial to two of his daughters by Peckitt himself. His *Commission Book* is the earliest surviving account of glass painting and includes 315 works ranging from sash windows to cathedral windows.

## Petergate

Follows the route of the Roman *Via Principalis* and is named after the **Minster**.

Peter Prison – an 1895 drawing by G. H. Fowler Jones (from an earlier picture) showing the Peter Prison through the Peter Gate archway (on the corner of High Petergate and what is now Duncombe Place).

## Peter Prison

The origins of the prison and the Minster Police date from 1106 when the Liberty of St Peter and Peter Prison was formed and appointed its own constables separate from the rest of the city of York. Today there are ten **Minster Police**; they do not carry batons or handcuffs: their role is to look after over 380 sets of keys, to provide tourist information; security for cash and fire protection. The main part of the prison was the court, or Hall of Pleas. Peter Prison was reached through Peter Gate, one of four gates leading in to Minster Close or the Liberty of St Peter, a walled area around the **Minster**; it was demolished in 1827. **Jonathan Martin** was one of the last detainees, by which time a report found it in 'a wretched state'. The other three gates were at Ogleforth, the entrance to **St William's College** and at Minster Gates.

## Philippa of Hainault

Philippa of Hainault, a fifteen-year-old princess, who spoke both Flemish and French, came to York to marry **Edward III** on 24 January 1328. Queen Philippa often travelled with her husband, and was present at the defeat of the Scots at the Battle of Neville's Cross (1346) and the capture of Calais (1347), where she pleaded for the lives of the Six Burghers, shown in Rodin's marvellous sculpture in Calais (and its replica near the Houses of Parliament). Less well known is the fact that she successfully pleaded for the lives of the carpenters who had made a stand which collapsed at a tournament she attended in York. Queen's College, Oxford was founded in her honour. Hainault is in modern day Belgium.

## The Phoenix and the Black Babies

In George Street near Fishergate Bar, the original name until the mid 1800s was *The Labour in Vain*. The sign depicted a white woman scrubbing a black baby, in vain. The new name derives from the Phoenix Iron Foundry nearby.

## Plus ça Change

As the discussions over city centre and out of town retailing rumble on through the twenty-first century, it is instructive to quote a letter published in August 1790 in the *York Chronicle*: 'If the inhabitants of this city would rouse themselves to some spirited exertions and the Corporation open the gates to all tradesman and manufacturers inclinable to settle amongst us, York might again lift up its head and recover its ancient consequence as a principal place of commerce.'

## The Poor Clares

The first convent of the Sisters of the Second Order of Saint Francis was in Hull Road in 1865; they moved to the obscure St Joseph's Monastery in Lawrence Street in 1873. Today they still live there behind 20-foot-high walls, get up at 5.00 a.m., live in silence, are vegetarians and cultivate a 6-acre garden. But now there is also 'Goldie', technology designed at Goldsmith's College which brings the twenty-first century right into this closed, mediaeval world. From 'Goldie' comes world news which allows the nuns to pray for the people they read about on the screen; something they have always done in a more general sort of way; today they can do so in a much more informed, focused way.

## The Press Gang Comes to York

The Impress Service arrived in York on 18 January 1777 'to beat up for volunteers'. So angry were sections of the community that a letter was soon sent to the **Lord Mayor** threatening to burn down the **Mansion House** if the gang was not expelled. A reward of 100 guineas was offered for conviction of the author or authors and a twelve man guard was put on the Mansion House. Some ill disposed citizens used the presence of the press gang as an opportunity for revenge: to rid themselves of enemies by reporting scandalous and incriminating stories to the Lieutenant; or to benefit financially by posing as the press gang, seizing men and extorting money from their families for release. The real gang departed on 14 February 'having picked up a great Number of hands for His Majesty's Service', as reported in the *York Courant*.

## 'Pricke of Conscience' or Doom Window

The so-called Doom Window in **All Saints**, North Street. The dramatic 1410 window is an apocalyptic vision of a world on fire, as in the last fifteen days of the world before the Day of Judgement, and is as vivid a depiction of mediaeval terror and God-fearing repentance as you are likely to see anywhere. The captions are paraphrased (in English, not Latin) from the mediaeval poem, *The Pricke of Conscience* – unusual for the time in view of literacy levels amongst congregations and the prevalence of Latin in ecclesiatical settings. To some degree it is counter-balanced by the 'Corporal Acts of Mercy' window. The Acts of Mercy include feeding the hungry, offering drink to the thirsty, clothing the naked, visiting the sick and visiting those in prison, as in St Matthew's gospel.

## The Printer's Devil, Minerva and an American Indian

Staying with things Satanic, The 'Printer's Devil' effigy at 33 **Stonegate** at the corner of Coffee Yard has been looking down on us there since the 1880s and signifies the importance and prevalence of the **printing, bookselling** and **publishing** industries in the area. A printer's devil was a printer's apprentice, a factotum. Printing was commonly known as 'the black art' on account of the inks. The Devil is indicative of the common practice of denoting one's trade with a symbol – other examples are at 74a Petergate: the wonderful cigar shop native American Indian complete with headdress from around 1800, and the Minerva, at the corner of Minster Gates indicating a bookseller. Just as fascinating is the metal horse's head below the Indian whose nostrils used to flare with gas jets to provide a light for customers and passers-by. The reason for all this symbolism was simply that, at the time, most people could not read: even by 1870 one in three York women and one in five men could neither read nor write – so written signs were often useless; the practice declined somewhat from 1760 when they were outlawed and when house numbering and literacy increased.

Printing in full swing at the Herald Printing Works in 1934.

## Printing and Publishing in York

Printing came to England in 1477 with William Caxton and is first recorded in York in 1497 when Fridericus Freez, an immigrant 'docheman' is noted as 'Book Bynder' and 'Stationer' and later as a 'Buke Printer'. Hugo Goez set up in 1509 and Thomas Gent (d. 1778) published scores of chap books from Coffee Yard. **Grace White** was the first woman to publish a newspaper here in 1718, *The York Mercury,* in Coffee Yard with Thomas Hammond, **Quaker bookseller**; the paper passed to Thomas Gent in 1724. Another Quaker, **William Alexander,** opened a **bookselling** business in Castlegate in 1811 expanding into printing in 1814. This was eventually taken over by William Sessions in 1865, surviving until 2009. Ben Johnson and Co Ltd was established as a lithographic printer by Johnson and John Lancaster, specialising in railway timetables and other jobs associated with the railways. John Glaisby's bookshop and library was in **Coney Street**; in 1848 it had been the premises of William Hargrove's *York Herald*, next to the George Hotel and known then as Kidd's Coffee House. Hargrove bought it from Caesar Ward, owner of the 1750 established Whig *York Courant*, in 1815; the *Courant* had been moved there from the **Bagnio** by Ann Ward, Caesar's widow. The magnificent statues and the bust and books have sadly gone although the publishing heritage of the building was extended when it became the offices of the then *York Evening Press* (1882) and the *Yorkshire Gazette and Herald* (which changed from a weekly in 1874 and absorbed the *Courant* in 1848). Ward was also the publisher of the first edition of **Laurence Sterne's** *The Life and Opinions of Tristram Shandy.* **FR Delittle,** at the Eboracum Letter Factory, in Railway Street was founded in 1888.

Priory Street – the entrance to the Benedictine Monastery in Micklegate removed in 1854 to allow Priory Street to be built.

## Priory Street

Rose from the destruction visited on the Priory of Benedictines in Micklegate to become, ironically perhaps, a centre for non-conformism with places of worship for Wesleyans, Baptists and Presbyterians springing up there. The Benedictines had come from the Abbey of St Martin of Marmoutier near Tours. The Priory was converted into tenements and 'ruthlessly demolished ... a monument of the ancient grandeur of our venerable city'.

## The Prison Walls

These were built in 1825 along Tower Street and demolished in the 1930s; they enclosed the Debtor's Prison and the Female Prison – both now occupied by the **Castle Museum** which has a section devoted, appropriately, to prison life. **Defoe**, with the distinct advantage of seeing things from the outside, liked the prison, describing it as 'the most stately and complete of any in the whole kingdom, if not in Europe'. The cells in which prisoners like **Dick Turpin** spent their last days before execution can be visited (with impunity) ; Turpin was hanged for horse stealing in 1739. A First World War tank stood sentinel in Tower Gardens for many years as a memorial to the War – before it was melted down in the Second World War for scrap.

## Pump Court

At the junction of King's Court and Newgate, Pump Court was the site of one of the many water pumps and wells that served the city. Piped water was turned on in parts of the city between 1677 and 1685; a public bathhouse opened in 1691. John Wesley preached in a room (the 'Oven') here in 1753 (one of twenty-six visits to the city); it became an official place of worship for Methodists in 1754. One of the country's only two surviving lantern tower windows is in Pump Court, tragically, almost hidden from public view. Betty Petre lived here; she kept her cattle in the court before slaughter in **Shambles**; Mr Huber collected sheeps' guts and washed them in a drain before exporting them to Germany to make fiddle strings. Other residents included a chimney sweep and a prostitute, referred to locally as 'an old knock'.

## Quakers

By 1850 the Society of Friends was relatively well established in York with a Meeting House in Castlegate, moving in 1886 to Clifford Street, a burial ground in Bishophill and two schools – **Bootham** for boys and **The Mount** for girls. There was also a network of Adult Schools throughout the city, at which John and **Joseph Rowntree** were the first teachers, and regular Monthly and Quarterly Meetings. Membership in York was 200 in 1855 rising to 543 in 1915. Social welfare extended beyond care of the poor and the promotion of tolerance to the humane and civilized treatment of the mentally ill at **The Retreat.**

## Quakers and Chocolate

There is an inextricable association between English chocolate manufacturing and the Society of Friends, or Quakerism. Fry, Cadbury, **Rowntree** and Thorne of Leeds were

The Multangular Tower.

all Quakers. Why was it that the chocolate industry at the end of the nineteenth century and in the early years of the twentieth prospered largely under Quaker ownership? It is all the more remarkable, though, when we remember that in 1851 Quakers accounted for less than 0.1 per cent of the 21 million population of England. Friends were excluded from the only teaching universities in England at the time, Oxford and Cambridge, because of their non-conformism and the universities' association with Anglicanism; they were debarred from Parliament and the guilds; they were restricted in what they could and could not do as lawyers because they refused to take oaths; the arts were considered frivolous and they were disqualified from the armed services because they were usually pacifists. One of the few alternatives left to well to do young Quakers was to pursue a life in industry or business, and this is what many did. In doing so they often brought with them a tradition of high quality management and fair trading practices, rigorous scientific research and innovative technical development as well as a preoccupation with quality and a breathtakingly detailed attention to commercial administration. So Quakers entered business and industry: one of the emerging industries at the time was cocoa and chocolate – this was partly a result of increased affordability amongst the working classes who had more disposable income, lower taxes on imports which reduced prices in the shops, and improvements in quality, a better taste and less adulteration. What had been a luxury for the few was fast becoming an affordable indulgence for many. Moreover, cocoa and chocolate dovetailed perfectly with Quaker views on temperance; they were healthy beverages too, because their consumption entailed boiling what was often unclean water. One of the legacies of the frequent Meetings routinely held by Quakers to spread the word was the building up of a strong network of dependable friends and contacts; this in turn, along with intermarriage amongst Quaker families, led to a tradition of mutual assistance and an ethical, enlightened attitude in business and industry, and to strong industrial partnerships, underpinned by unfaltering service and philanthropy to the community at large. All of this manifested itself in York through Rowntree's; as such Quakerism has had an immeasurable effect on the city in every way – commercially, socially, educationally and physically – for over a century.

## Queen Margaret's Arch

Named after **Margaret Tudor**, who stayed in York in 1503 on her way to marry James IV of Scotland. Adjacent to the **Bar Walls** opposite the **King's Manor**, it was built in 1497 as a short cut to and from St Mary's Abbey for use by Henry VII for 'his pleasure and passage to the Mynster'.

## Railfest – York 800

This unique railway festival brought together for the first time ever a number of record-breaking locomotives all of which have left their stamp on rail history for being the fastest, largest, strongest, first, last or oldest. They include the fastest steam locomotive (126 mph) *Mallard*, the newest functioning mainline steam locomotive, *Tornado*, the UK's most powerful industrial steam locomotive, *Mardy Monster* and restored *Flying Scotsman*, the first locomotive to reach 100 mph. There is also an array of strange railway vehicles including a sail powered 'engine'. The festival is a fitting testament to York's railway heritage.

Aerial view of York Railway Station and the hotel.

## The Railways

The railway king, **George Hudson,** was prominent in York's development as a major railway city; his advice to George Stephenson was to make it a hub: 'Mak all t'railways cum t'York'. The first train left York for South Milford in 1839. The first London service was in 1840 via Derby or Birmingham and took about eleven hours. In 1841 the industry in York employed forty-one people; this rose to 513 by 1851 (390 of whom were from out of town bringing 537 dependents); by the end of the century NER employed 5500 workers in York, about half in the carriage works. In the 1850s the railway replaced the five or so stagecoaches per day between London and York which started in 1703 (carrying 24,000 passengers per year, six per coach, and taking four to six days depending on the weather) with thirteen trains carrying 341,000 passengers. The fare to London via Grantham in 1882 was 33s 4d (I class), 25s 4d (II class – equal to about 1 week's wages for a semi-skilled man). 15s 8d (III class). By 1888 there were 294 trains arriving at the station each day: this all led to a marked rise in York's tourist industry; it also revolutionised communications.  By the mid-1860s York had two daily postal deliveries; a letter posted in London before noon was delivered in York later the same evening! York's main post office in Lendal was built in 1884. The emerging confectionery industry with **Rowntrees, Terry's** and **Craven's** also benefitted enormously. The **River Ouse** had been the main transport route before the railways came ; *White's 1840 Directory* was highly optimistic about the benefits of railways in the future: 'The formation of railways to open a better communication with the West of Yorkshire and the North and South of England, are in progress and with these improved modes of transit for goods, it is to be hoped that the trade of York will improve.' The next development was carriage

York's second railway station from the Bar Walls in the 1850s

York's third, and current, railway
station in the 1890s.

and wagon construction – all of which moved to a 45-acre site at Holgate; the railways
were York's first large scale industry and its biggest employer. In 2012 **Railfest**, Britain's
biggest railway event formed part of York 800.

## Railway Stations in York

York has had three railway stations. The first was a temporary wooden building on
Queen Street outside the walls, opened in 1839 by the York & North Midland Railway.
It was replaced in 1841, on Tanner Row within the walls, by what is now called the
old York railway station and was built by Robert Stephenson on land owned by Lady
Hewley's Charity **almshouses**. Scawin's Railway Hotel opened the same year; it was
demolished in 1900. The King of Saxony and **Charles Dickens** were amongst travellers
arriving here. The buildings were reminiscent of Euston Station in Euston Square.
Access was difficult, from North Street, and this eventually led to the construction
of Hudson Street (after **George Hudson**), and **Lendal Bridge**. Because through trains
between London and Newcastle needed to reverse out of George Hudson's old York
station in order to continue their journey, a new station was built outside the walls.
This is the present station, designed by the North Eastern Railway architects Thomas
Prosser and William Peachey, which opened in 1877. It had thirteen platforms and
was at that time the largest station in the world. At 800 feet long and 234 feet wide it

The Red House with Tate Wilkinson's house next door; the passage in between led to the old entrance to the Theatre Royal. The flambeau extinguisher is still at the doorway of the Red House. From an illustration by R. Grundy Heape in his *Georgian York*.

is one of the most spectacular examples of railway architecture in the world, rightly and famously described as 'A splendid monument of extravagance', and 'York's propylaeum'. As part of the new station project, the **Royal Station Hotel** (now The Royal York Hotel), designed by Peachey, opened in 1878.

## Raindale Mill – Mill on the Foss
An early nineteenth-century flour mill removed from Raindale, Newton on the North York Moors to the grounds of the **York Castle Museum** in 1965, close to the **River Foss**.

## The Red House
Dates from 1718 – its candle snuffer can still be seen; **Dr John Burton** (*Tristram Shandy's* Dr Slop) once lived there; it is now an antiques centre. Burton was a gynaecologist and medical author whose books included *An Essay Towards a Complete System of Midwifery*, illustrated by no less an artist than George Stubbs who had come to York (then, as now, a centre of excellence in medical science) to learn his anatomy. Stubbs found work teaching medical students in the **Medical School** before taking up comparative anatomy, and painting his famous horses. His most celebrated, *Whistlejacket*, was painted in 1762 and featured the very same horse that won the 4-mile chase for 2,000 guineas at the **Knavesmire** in August 1759.

The Red Tower.

### The Red Tower
The Red Tower (named after the colour of its brickwork – all the other walls, bars and towers being built with Tadcaster limestone) is just off Foss Islands Road. Its walls are 4 feet thick. The tower was built around 1490 by Henry VII and restored in 1857 after being damaged in the Civil War siege of York. The original roof was flat and it boasted a projecting toilet. It was also known as Brimstone House when it was used as a gunpowder warehouse; around 1800 it was a stables.

### The Resurrection Men or Jerry Crunchers
Instances of body snatching and burking (after Burke and Hare where victims are murdered for their cadavers) abound in York – partly because the city was on the main coach route to Edinburgh and its famous medical school. Even after the passing of the Anatomy Act in 1832 which legalised the trafficking of the bodies of lunatics and paupers between Poor Law Unions and medical schools, the 'unhallowed occupation' continued here – probably due to the opening of York's first **medical school**. *The York Courant* of 14 January 1834 reports that in St Saviourgate 'one Matthew Joy when questioned ... stated that he merely wanted a skull for a person who had applied to him for one , in order to pulverise it, and mix it with some treacle, to give it to a person who was subject to fits'.

### The Retreat
In 1796 **William Tuke** founded The Retreat in York, in which he instigated a revolutionary way of treating the mentally ill: namely, humanely. This was in stark

contrast to existing methods which saw patients as possessed by demons, chaining them up as criminals: prisoners rather than patients in a squalid, punitive environment. Tuke wanted 'an institution for the care and proper treatment of those labouring under that most afflictive dispensation, the loss of reason.' His resolve was triggered when the relatives of a Quaker patient, Hannah Mills, were refused visiting rights to the York **Lunatic Asylum** after Hannah's death there; Hannah had been kept shackled. A delegation of Quakers obtained permission to visit and inspect. The thirty-bed Retreat was the result: 'a habitation for persons in a state of lunacy', and it laid the foundations for the modern treatment of psychiatric disorders and patients. In 1813 Samuel Tuke described it as 'moral treatment' in his *Description of the Retreat*. The Retreat continues to serve the needs of the psychiatric patient today and remains a highly respected centre of excellence. Another legacy of William's was the establishment of Trinity Lane Girl's School, later to become the **Mount School**; their motto is *fidelis in parvo*.

## Richard III
Born in 1452 Richard was King from 1483 until his death in 1485 in the Battle of Bosworth Field . Last king of the House of York and the last of the Plantagenets he was always a friend of the city of York and the people of York repaid him with affection, military support and respect. In 1483 Richard allowed York to elect four MPs instead of the usual two, only London had the same privilege, and established the King's Council of the North here, which effectively meant a devolved government for the north of England based in York. As President, Richard came often to York, staying at the Augustinian Friary in Lendal, between what is now the **Guildhall** and **Lendal Bridge**. His memory is currently preserved in the Richard III Museum at **Monk Bar**.

## Ridsdale Tate, E.
Born in York in 1862, died 1922. Ridsdale Tate designed the anchorage attached to **All Saints, North Street** (1910) and the Tempest Anderson Hall at the **Yorkshire Museum**. In 1915 he was commissioned by the *York Herald* to draw a panoramic bird's eye view of York as it was in the fifteenth century to celebrate the 20,000th copy of the *York Gazette*; it was published on 18 May 1915. He also illuminated the pages and designed the oak boards and silver clasps for the *King's Book of York Fallen Heroes* presented to Prince Albert, Duke of York in 1920 and to be held in perpetuity in the Minster.

## River Foss
In 1069 William the Conqueror dammed the River Foss near to its confluence with the **Ouse** to create a moat around the castle; this caused the river to flood upstream and form a large lake known as the King's Pool or the King's Fish Pond. King's Pool was an integral feature of the city's inner defences during the Middle Ages – the marsh was virtually impassable and explains why there is no city wall between Layerthorpe Postern and the **Red Tower**. **Roman** jetties, wharves and warehouses have been excavated on the river banks, indicating that water-borne transport and trade was important from Roman times. Foss Bridge, at the end of Walmgate, dates from 1811 and replaces a 1403 stone bridge and a wooden one before that. The fish shambles was

River Ouse at King's Staithe in the 1940s.

The River Ouse at New Walk in the 1930s with Ouse Bridge and Terry's on the left in Clementhorpe, and the Crimea cannons in the centre.

*Vue sur l'Ouse près de York*, a watercolour by Henry Gastineau (1792-1876) in York City Art Gallery.

here as was the Saturday pig market (the tethering rings still exist) and the goose fair. There was a Chicory Works near **Jewbury** which processed the chicory which grew to the north east of the city.

## River Ouse

The **Romans** called it *Isis*, the Saxons *Youre* and *Eurewic*. It often froze over in the early years of the twentieth century and skating on the river was very popular. The ice is said to have been up to twelve inches thick at times. Apart from skating, horse chestnut sellers set up braziers and stalls on the ice; there were even horse races between the Tower and Marygate in 1740 and football matches in 1607. Racing is mentioned in Edward Baines' 1823 *History and Gazetteer of York*: 'In 1607, there was a frost of such severity and continuance that the Ouse became almost a solid body of ice and a horse race was run on the river from the Tower at the end of Marygate, under the great arch of the bridge, to the crane at Skeldergate postern.' In 1740 **Thomas Gent** set up his printing press on the ice, producing a leaflet to celebrate the event. There is a ship's figurehead in **Stonegate** where this and ships' timbers, with which some of the city's buildings were made, reveal York's history as a port. The Ouse Navigation Trustees built the slipway at Clementhorpe in 1836which gives its name to the pub there, *The Slipway*. The Festival of the Rivers with its flotilla on the river is one of the celebrations in York 800.

The column celebrating the VI Victrix legion.

### Robin Hood's Tower

On the walls between **Bootham** and **Monk Bar**; named probably for no other reason, like *The Robin Hood* pub in **Castlegate**, than that Robin Hood and what he stood for was 'a good thing'. The existing tower is an 1899 replacement.

### The Roman Bath, St Sampson's Square

Formerly *The Mail Coach*, *The Barrel Churn*, *The Cooper*, *The Barrel*, the Roman bathhouse excavated here in 1930 is partly visible, including cold room: *frigidarium*, hot room: *caldarium* and underfloor central heating system: *hypocaust*. Tiles stamped *Legio VI* and *Legio IX* have been uncovered recording which legions were stationed at *Eboracum*.

### Roman York

*Eboracum* was occupied by the Romans from AD 71 until AD 410 when they left Britannia for good. Quintus Petilius Cerialis led the IX Hispana Legion north to subdue the Brigantes and established a garrison here. Strategically York was of major significance, being of considerable military importance and a major communications centre. The Colonia covered 60 acres and the walls were 20 feet high and 4 feet thick in parts. The *Praetorium* is under the **Minster**, there is an amphitheatre and temple under **Micklegate** and a *forum basilica* , baths on the banks of the **Ouse**, a sewerage system in Bishophill, a VI Victrix Legion column opposite the Minster and a statue of **Constantine** nearby to celebrate his being proclaimed Emperor here in AD 306 on the death of his father, the

Emperor Constantius Chlorus in York, and his conversion to Christianity, probably in 312. Septimius Severus, Rome's first black emperor, lived in York between 208 and 211; his sons, Caracalla and Geta, were declared co-Emperors in 198 and 209. Severus died in York in 211 and received a spectacular funeral in the city, but not before he had declared York to be the capital of Britannia Inferior. Hadrian visited too.

## The Rose Window

Twenty-two feet in diameter, the magnificent Rose Window was badly damaged by the fire on 9 July 1984 . The Minster is home to one of the largest collections of stained glass in Britain with 128 windows containing two million pieces of glass. Each one is cleaned and restored every 125 years; they are each taken apart and every piece of glass is cleaned individually. The Rose Window tracery dates from about 1240 with most of the glass from about 1500; its red and white Tudor roses celebrate the end of the Wars of the Roses. It was once known as the Wheel Window, and the Marigold Window, from the flower in the middle. This is now a sunflower painted by **William Peckitt** in 1793. The heat from the 1984 fire created about 40,000 cracks in the glass which glaziers spent two and a half years repairing and restoring to the brilliance we see today.

## Rowntree, Benjamin Seebohm

Benjamin Seebohm (1871-1954), Seebohm was his mother's German family name, joined the family firm in 1888; he had graduated in chemistry from Owen's College at the University of Manchester. Among his many achievements at Rowntree was establishing the company's first laboratory in 1897 and  appointing the firm's first

The Rowntree grocer shop in Pavement in the 1920s, then run by T. Coning.

food chemist, Samuel H. Davies, another **Quaker**. He is, nevertheless, equally well known for his pioneering work on urban poverty and the plight of the poor in his ground-breaking and influential *Poverty: A Study of Town Life*, a book which helped lay the foundations for the modern welfare state. A friend of David Lloyd George's, he is credited with informing the Old Age Pensions Act (1908) and the National Insurance Act (1911). He describes **Hungate** as typical of urban slum life while all too mindful of the many individual, prudent, exceptions to the rule: 'reckless expenditure of money as soon as obtained, with the aggravated want at other times; the rowdy Saturday night, the Monday morning pilgrimage to the pawn shop ... the despair of so many social workers'. His later works included *Poverty and Progress* (1941) and *Poverty and the Welfare State* (1951). Seebohm lived at the Homestead in Clifton until 1936 which is now occupied by the Joseph Rowntree Foundation; the grounds have always been open to the public.

## Rowntree, Henry Isaac (1838-1883)
Bought **William Tuke's** cocoa business to found **Rowntree's** in 1862.

## Rowntree, John Stephenson (1834-1907)
**Lord Mayor** in 1880-1881 and founder of York's first **Quaker** Adult School in Hope Street, off Walmgate. In 1857 it moved to **Lady Peckett's Yard**, behind the **Rowntree's Pavement** shop.

## Rowntree I, Joseph
The elder Joseph Rowntree came to York from Scarborough where his father ran a grocer's shop and where Joseph had worked since he was eleven. Joseph too became a grocer with a shop in Pavement; its apprentices included George Cadbury. He bought the **Pavement** shop in 1822 on his twenty-first birthday, at an auction at *The Elephant & Castle Inn* in Skeldergate ; the auctioneer was so drunk that Joseph and his friend, James Backhouse, had to plunge his head in a sobering barrel of cold water so that the sale could proceed. Rowntree Senior was a tough boss; one of his uncompromising memoranda perhaps reveals how and why the family businesses succeeded: 'The object of the Pavement establishment is business. The young men who enter it ... are expected to contribute ... in making it successful ... it affords a full opportunity for any painstaking, intelligent young man to obtain a good practical acquaintance with the tea and grocery trades ... the place is not suitable for the indolent and wayward.' Apart from his enduring success in confectionery, Joseph was a tireless worker in other, Quaker-related fields. These included York **County Hospital**, the York **Dispensary**, the Bible Society, the Religious Tract Society, the City Mission, the York Female Penitentiary and the York Soup Kitchen. He was elected **Mayor** in 1858 but refused it on religious grounds on payment of a £100 fine. He died in 1859.

## Rowntree II, Joseph
The **Pavement** shop was to give Joseph's son, the younger Joseph Rowntree, a sound and invaluable seventeen year apprenticeship in retail and business management. This,

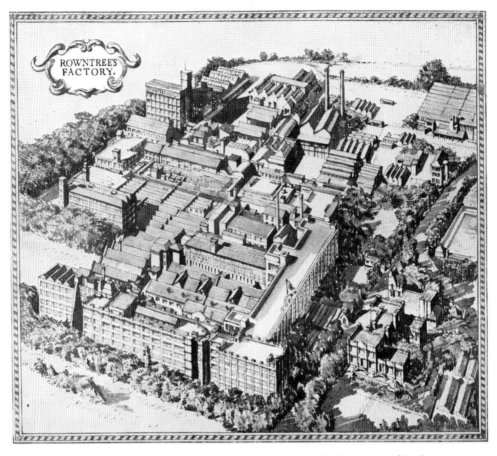

'The history of Rowntree & Co Ltd is intimately bound up with the history of York.'

and an earlier period of work as a wholesale grocer's near Fenchurch Street in London from 1857, provided a priceless foundation for the next stage of his career when he joined his brother, Henry at the cocoa works in Tanner's Moat.

## Rowntree's

In July 1862 **Henry Isaac Rowntree** (who had served his apprenticeship both at the family shop in **Pavement** and at **Tuke's**) bought the Tuke's grocery in **Castlegate**; it specialised in tea, cocoa and chocolate. Henry relocated the firm to an old foundry at Tanner's Moat in 1864. In 1869 he was joined by his brother, **Joseph Rowntree** II, and the firm H. I. Rowntree & Co was established. Joseph brought much needed business acumen to the company and focused on the financial and sales side leaving the manufacturing to Henry. A sales call by Claude Gaget in 1879 had a major impact on Rowntrees. Gaget was working for Compagnie Française, Parisian confectioners, in London. The samples of gums and pastilles he presented that day eventually led to Rowntrees' manufacture in 1881 of their famous *Crystallized Gum Pastilles*. The success of fruit pastilles and fruit gums enabled Joseph to invest in new machinery in 1880, notably a van Houten press for the production in York of cocoa essence – *Rowntrees Elect*, made from top quality cocoa. Joseph bought a 20-acre site on Haxby Road in 1890 with a view to building a more efficient and ergonomic factory which would enable the firm to meet the growing demand for their products.

## Rowntree Park

The City of York benefitted from **Joseph Rowntree's** sense of civic responsibility and philanthropy when in 1909 the Yearsley Road swimming baths next to the Haxby Road factory were donated to the people of York. Rowntree Park was given to York by Rowntree in 1921 at the end of the First World War as a memorial to the company's staff who lost their lives or suffered during the War. The park was York's first municipal park. A set of gates were added to the park in memory of those who fell in the Second World War. Bronze plaques mark both occasions within the Lych Gate. Situated, somewhat ironically, on Terry Avenue, on the banks of the **River Ouse**, the 30-acre park has recently benefitted from a £1.8 million refurbishment restoring it to its original beauty.

## The Royal Mint

The first mint in York was set up under the Saxons, producing coins up until the Norman period. The Royal Mint at York was established in St Leonard's in 1279 to relieve the overworked London mint, particularly for the production of farthings. It closed in 1280 and reopened in 1300. Both Edward III and Charles I established Royal Mints in the city.

Royal Station Hotel with horse-powered taxis.

## The Royal Press
Charles I set up his **printing** press in 1642 in Sir Henry Jenkins' house in **St Williams' College.** The royal presses rolled from March to August that year and turned out seventy-four documents including Charles' *Counsell of Warre.*

## The Royal Station Hotel
Part of the new station project, the Station Hotel opened in 1878 under the management of LNER. A five-storey building of yellow Scarborough brick, it featured elegant, high-ceilinged banqueting rooms and 100 large bedrooms for fourteen shillings a night. The twenty-seven room west wing was added in 1896, named Klondyke after the US gold rush. The hotel was later renamed *The Royal York* after a visit by Victoria en route to Balmoral. This was York's second Royal Station Hotel, the first had been next to the second station.

## Scarborough Bridge
The bridge is a T-girder built in 12 weeks in 1845 to the design of Robert Stephenson costing £3,918 1*d.* It catered for foot and rail: originally pedestrians had to walk between the two tracks; the entrance was later bricked up and a safer footpath constructed. A bridge of similar construction in Chester collapsed in 1847.

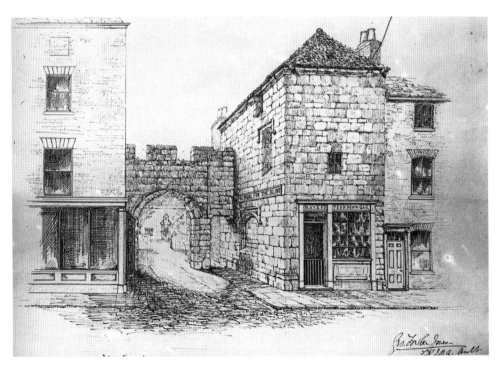

Sketch of Old Gateway in Bootham leading to Blind School.

## The School for the Blind

The Wilberforce Memorial was the charity behind the Yorkshire School for the Blind; it was established in the King's Manor on the death of William Wilberforce in 1833 out of a desire to honour his memory and good works in as fitting a manner as possible. Wilberforce had represented Yorkshire as an MP for twenty-eight years and was an influential voice not just for the movement to abolish the slave trade but also for the education and training of the blind. The School's mission was: 'To provide sound education together with instruction in manual training and technical work, for blind pupils, between the ages of five and twenty; to provide employment in suitable workshops or homes for a limited number of blind men and women who've lost their sight after the age of sixteen, in some occupation carried on at the school; and to promote such other agencies for the benefit of the blind as may enable them to gain their livelihood, or spend a happy old age.'

## The School of Art

Opened in Minster Yard in 1842 as a branch of the Normal School of Design in London with the help of **William Etty**. Originally in the Freemasons' Hall in Little Blake Street it moved into the former premises of **St Peter's School** in Minster Yard in 1848, moving again to the Exhibition Building in St Leonard's Place and again to Marygate in 1949 where the roll was 594 students.

Shambles from King's Square – this wonderful card shows Christ Church (or Holy Trinity) in 1871, and points out that is the only church where you can see three sides at the same time, due to its trapezoidal shape. After 1886 it was redundant and used as a cattle pen.

## Scrope, Archbishop

Executed in 1405 by Henry IV for his rebellion after his, Henry Bolingbroke's, 1399 victory over **Richard III**. Henry marched on York, determined to 'wipe it off the face of the earth'. Miracles were seen in the **Minster** which led to Henry banning all services for a year; his death from leprosy in 1413 was seen as divine retribution for the murder of an **archbishop**.

## Shambles

Mentioned in the *Domesday* the Latin name for Shambles is *in Macello*. Along with nearby **Whipmawhopmagate** perhaps one of the most famous streets in the world and the most visited street in Europe. In 2010 it won the *Google Britain's Most Picturesque Street Award*. Shambles was originally called Haymongergate to signify the hay that was here to feed the livestock before slaughter; after that it was called Needlergate after the needles made here from the bones of slaughtered animals. It gets its present name (at first The Great Flesh Shambles) from the fleshammels – a shammel being the wooden board butchers used to display their meat on. They would throw their past-sell-by-date meat, offal, blood and guts into the runnel in the middle of the street to add to the mess caused by chamber pot disposal from the overhanging jetties . Now you know what a real shambles really is. In 1280 seventeen butchers paid an annual shammel toll of seventy shillings between them; in 1872 twenty-five out of the thirty-nine shops here were butchers out of a total of eighty-eight in the whole of York. There were also four pubs: *The Globe* (closed 1936); *The Eagle and Child* (closed 1925); *The Neptune* (closed 1903) and *The Shoulder of Mutton* (closed 1898). The street is narrow by design, to keep the sun off the meat.

Skeldergate Bridge.

## Skeldergate Bridge

The castle-like building here was a tollhouse; the fee to cross, up to 1914 when tolls were ended, was ½d. Work on the bridge began in 1875; it opened in 1881 at a cost of £56,000 – 40 per cent over budget, replacing the ferry which was used by around 800 people each day. The bridge had an opening mechanism which has now been immobilised.

## Slavery in York

A slave market is said to have existed in **St Sampson's Square** during the Roman occupation. Later, Bede tells us that Pope Gregory I (d. 604) admired English slaves, punning *'non Angli sed angeli'* – 'they're not Angles, but angels'. More recently in 1909 the use of slave labour on cocoa plantations became a controversial and embarrassing ethical issue for the chocolate industry, particularly Fry, Cadbury and **Rowntree**, philanthropists and **Quakers** all. Despite legislation, the use of what was effectively state sanctioned slave labour continued in West Africa – a major source of raw materials for the chocolate makers; the outcome of reports from the Quaker Joseph Buritt and Henry Nevison for *Harper's Weekly* was that all three companies would boycott cocoa from Portuguese colonial São Thome and Príncipé.

## Snickelways

The network of narrow pedestrian-only alleyways which spider their way across the city. The word is a neologism coined by Mark Jones in his 1983 *A Walk Around the Snickelways of York*; it is a compound of <u>snicket</u>, a walled passageway ; <u>ginnel</u>, a narrow passageway between buildings, and *alleyway*, a narrow street or lane. In York, examples include **Mad Alice Lane**, Hornpot Lane, **Mucky Peg Lane**, Hole in the Wall, Pope's Head Alley, and Coffee Yard (Langton Lane). *The Snickleway* (*sic*) Inn in Goodramgate was originally called *The Anglers* because it was close to the **Minster** stonemasons' yard – an angler being a geometrist working on the stones. This follows a long tradition of being named after artisans: previous names also include *The Painters' Arms, The Square & Compass* and *The Board*.

## Snow, Dr John

Celebrated physician born 1813 in North Street, Snow was a pioneer in anesthesia: he correctly calculated dosages of chloroform and ether as an anesthetic. He was the anesthetist at the birth of Queen Victoria's last of nine children, Beatrice Mary Victoria Feodore, born in 1856 and later Princess Beatrice of Battenberg.

## Sterne, Laurence

Sterne (1713-1768) is famous for his *The Life and Opinions of Tristram Shandy, Gentleman*, and *A Sentimental Journey Through France and Italy*; he was also an Anglican clergyman with a vicarship at Sutton-on-the-Forest, a living at Stillington and was a prebendary of **York Minster,** lodging at **Hildyard's** in **Stonegate**. Sterne married Elizabeth Lumley who lived in College Street. His satire *A Political Romance* (1759), exposed political infighting at the Minster. Sterne died of pleurisy in London in 1768; he is buried in the churchyard in Coxwold, but only after a circuitous journey ... having been originally interred in St George's churchyard, Hanover Square, London. His body was snatched by '**resurrection men**' for use in medical dissection at Cambridge University. The cadaver was recognised by the Professor of Anatomy there who fainted when he saw it on the table and had it hastily reburied. In 1969 the Lawrence Sterne Society obtained permission to remove Sterne's remains to Coxwold for re-burial .

## St Andrew's

In Spen Lane; it has a fifteenth-century timber roof and is the only survivor of the churches made redundant at the Reformation, at one time converted into a stable at one end and into a brothel at the other. It was also one of the many homes of **St Peter's School** and is now the home of the York Brethren Assembly.

## St Anthony's Hall

The Hall was built in Peaseholme Green between 1446 and 1453 on the site of a chapel of St Anthony for either the Guild of St Martin or the Guild of St Anthony of Vienna (which was founded in 1446). Henry VIII and Katherine Howard were entertained here. After the demise of the Guilds, it was used between 1627 and 1705 variously as a Royalist arsenal, a military and a plague hospital and a prison. When the **Blue Coat School** closed in

Early nineteenth-century Pavement showing the Market Cross (demolished in the 1830s) and St Crux church (demolished in the 1890s) – it would be hard to find two similar acts of such crass civic vandalism.

1947 it was used by the York Civic Trust and in 1953 became the Borthwick Institute for Historical Research, now the Borthwick Institute for Archives, at the **J. B. Morrell** Library at the **University of York**. The Quilt Museum and Gallery opened in the Hall in 2008.

## St Crux

One of the most heinous acts of Victorian civic vandalism to be visited on a city was the dynamiting of the cupola-topped St Crux in **Pavement** in 1887 on health and safety grounds. More happily, some of the church's treasures can be seen in the Parish Hall which was built from the rubble, not least the beautiful 1610 monuments to Sir Robert and Lady Margaret Watter. Watter was **Lord Mayor of York** in 1591 and 1603; he bestowed his gold chain of office on the city: 'conteyninge in weight xxtie ounce lack half a quarter or ther aboute' – it has been worn by every York Mayor since. Sir Robert gave James VI of Scotland breakfast on his march south.

## St George's Fields

Here was the York ducking stool – for scoundrels and women who sold short measures or bad beer and 'scolds and flyters'. The gallows nearby attracted large crowds, some coming by special train excursions as late as 1862. There were heated baths here from 1879 to 1972: they comprised separate men's and women's baths and a bath for York residents without a bath at home who could come and bathe there.

St Helen's Square – the 1816 Greek Revival Savings Bank from a wood engraving by Henry Brown originally published in *Eighty Three Views in York* printed by John Hill, Marygate, 1838. Facsimile published by G. H. Smith of Easingwold in 1976.

## St George's Super-Cinema

Opened in 1921 next to Fairfax House it could seat 1,340 viewers including 450 in the balcony. The screen was 22 by 18 feet; the orchestra was led by Harold Croke. The first film was *Three Men in a Boat*; seat prices ranged from 8*d* to 1*s* 6*d*.

## St Helen's Square

The square was purchased from St Helen's churchyard in 1703 to allow the gentry easier carriage access to the **Assembly Rooms** thus avoiding the messy and baneful graveyard. The church was actually being demolished in 1551 before it was reprieved and rebuilt. The 1876 lantern tower replaced a steeple. The maiden Davyes sisters, Barbara and Elizabeth, were buried here, both ninety-eight, and witnesses to seven monarchs from Charles II to George III. Their nephew, Theophylus Davyes Garencieres, was related to the eminent French physician Theophylus Garencieres (d. 1680). Davyes died of yellow fever in St Domingo in 1797. The Savings Bank was built in 1829, the Yorkshire Insurance Building in 1840.

## St John's Voluntary Secondary Modern School

The Practising School and the Model School of the **York and Ripon Diocesan Training College** were opened in 1851 and 1859 respectively in Lord Mayor's Walk. The two schools were complementary, the best teaching methods being illustrated in the Model School for the students who then put them into practice in the other. A new combined school building was built in 1899.

## St Leonard's Hospital

St Leonard's was one of the largest mediaeval hospitals in the north of England, built on the site of St Peters Hospital which was razed by fire in 1137. The charitable brief of the hospital brothers, who lived by rule of Austin canons, was to distribute daily alms at its gates to thirty poor people, give alms to prisoners in the city and to leper houses, and maintain 206 sick poor in the hospital until they were well enough to return to work. Staffed comprised thirteen brethren and eight sisters pursuing a quasi-monastic lifestyle. The replacement was destroyed in the Dissolution leaving York without a hospital until 1740. As was customary, the sick would not be treated until they had confessed their sins. The high ceilings and large windows of St Leonard's were not just for show or illumination: disease was thought to be caused by 'bad air'. Such ceilings and windows allowed fresh air to circulate and cure. The size of the hospital can be gauged from the fact that the **Theatre Royal** is built on part of the site, which extends to the undercroft and chapel still visible today.

## St Martin-cum-Gregory

Now redundant, it was mentioned in *Domesday*; much of the building in Micklegate is fourteenth and fifteenth century; the tower plinth is made from stone pillaged from the Roman Temple of Mithras, the tower is from 1844. The graveyard was always over full and in hot weather 'the exhalations from the graveyard have been distinctly felt in the street by passers by'. Henry Cave (d. 1836), author of *Antiquities of York*, is buried

St Mary's Abbey, *c.* 1910.

here. The **butter market** thrived here until 1838. At their peak, butter exports from York amounted to 80,000 firkins.

### St Martin le Grand

The church is now a moving shrine to all those who lost their lives in the two World Wars. The magnificent Great West Window (31 feet high and 13 feet wide) was prudently removed at the beginning of the Second World War and is now in the south aisle. **Margaret Clitherow** was married there two years before converting to Roman Catholicism.

### St Mary's Abbey

One of the richest abbeys in the country, the Benedictines completed it in 1088. The surrounding walls (originally three-quarters of a mile long) were built after townsfolk's attacks on the abbey when one of the clerics, Simon de Warwick, imposed taxes on the market along **Bootham,** outside the city walls. In 1132 Richard, the prior, and thirteen monks demanded a return to a traditionally simpler life which also involved giving away much of the abbey's money. After a near riot the rebels left York to found the much stricter Cistercian Fountains Abbey. Their departure had no impact on St Mary's decadence which was celebrated in the *Ballads of Robin Hood*, one of whose enemies is a 'ryche abbot here besyde of Seynt Mari Abbey'. The life-size stone saints and prophets painted in gold and other colours which adorned the west front of St Mary's Abbey church are now in the **Yorkshire Museum**. They included Moses adorned with horns, typical of the mediaeval period due to a mistranslation of the Hebrew Bible into the Latin Vulgate Bible. The Hebrew word taken from *Exodus* can mean either a 'horn' or an 'irradiation' and in this case should be the latter; the most famous horned Moses is Michelangelo's statue in the Church of San Pietro in Vincoli, Rome.

### St Mary's Tower

Built about 1325 the tower was used to store monastery records after the Dissolution in 1539. During the Civil War in 1644, however, the Earl of Manchester blew it up with a mine at the Battle of the Bowling Green; the documents which survived were salvaged by Richard Dodsworth and are now in the **Minster Library**. The tower has been rebuilt. A contemporary account by royalist Sir Henry Slingsby tells us that 'Manchester, who had his Quarters about Clifton & Huworth ... makes his approaches, works his mines under St Mary's tower without Botham barr, & rais'd a battery against ye manner Wall that led to ye orchard, he begins to play wth his Cannon & throws down peice of ye Wall. We fall to work & make it up with earth & sods; this happn'd in ye morning: at noon they spring ye mine under St Mary's tower, & blows up one part of it, which falling outwards made ye access more easy; Then some at ye breach, some wth Ladders, getts up & enters, near 500. Sr. Philip Biron ye had ye guard at ye place ... was unfortunately kill'd as he open'd ye doors into ye bowling green whither ye enemy was gotten...'

### St Maurice's, Monkgate

The first church here was demolished in 1875 to make way for a larger one, itself pulled down in 1967 when Lord Mayor's Walk was widened. Forty-one headstones remain from the graveyard which would always have been busy due to the proximity of the **County Hospital.** One of the stipulations of the hospital was that prospective patients must pay a deposit on admission to cover burial fees – refundable only if you walked out alive.

### St Peter's School

Founded by St Paulinus of York in the year AD 627 as St Peter's Grammar School along with the **Minster Song School** close to where **York Minster** now stands. St Peter's is one of the oldest schools in the world, Chengdu Shishi High School China (143 BC) and Jondi Shapour in Gundeshapur, Persia (AD 271) are the oldest; it is the third oldest school in England, after The King's School, Canterbury (597) and Rochester. Early teachers and alumni include St John of Beverley, Egbert ( a friend of Bede's), **Alcuin** and Albert the Wise. Fifty boarders lived in the almonry at **St Mary's Abbey** rent free in return for help with services at the abbey and at St Olave's church. The Harrying of the North saw the destruction of the original school along with much of the city. William I delegated Thomas of Bayeux to rebuild the Minster and the school which then stood where the Minster's nave is now. The Dissolution of the Abbey meant that the school moved again and boarders had to find alternative accommodation: a royal licence allowed the new Royal School of St Peter's to take over premises in the Horse Fair, near present day Lord Mayor's Walk. The school was destroyed in the Civil War and the dwindling number of pupils moved to **Bedern** followed by five years in the **Bagnio**, a Turkish Bath in **Coney Street**; in 1736 it moved again to **St Andrew's** Church where it remained until 1828. A move back to a new school, later to become the Minster Song School, was followed by an amalgamation in 1844 with the Proprietary School in Clifton built in 1838 where the school now stands – ironically on land which **Guy Fawkes** once owned. Later Old Peterites include Guy Fawkes; **Joseph Terry**, confectioner; Christopher Hill, Marxist historian; Harry Gration, TV presenter; and John Barry, film score composer of eleven *James Bond* soundtracks, *Midnight Cowboy,* Born Free and Out of Africa. The school marks 5 November by not burning a 'Guy' on the bonfire, in deference to Guy Fawkes.

## St Robert of Knaresborough

Knaresborough's once world-famous eccentric saint was born Robert Flower, in York, in about 1160. He came of a good family, his father and brother becoming **Mayor of York**, but he chose to lead the life of a religious hermit, wandering about the Knaresborough district, but eventually settling in the riverside cave near Grimbald Bridge, still to be seen. Robert lived on roots and barley-bread, drinking only water. He grew his own crops and, according to legend, tamed stags and harnessed them to his plough. Latin texts in prose and verse tell his story. Because he befriended the poor and lawbreakers he was often in conflict with the authorities. But King John made a pilgrimage to his cave in 1216, and was impressed by his piety; this was in spite of the fact that Robert, deep in prayer, had at first refused to be disturbed, and then asked the retinue to point out which one was the King. Robert died in 1218, and the Priory later built on land given by King John carried on the saint's tradition of helping prisoners. His healing miracles continued to be associated with St Robert's tomb (probably confused with St Robert's Well), visited by so many, including Edward I, from Knaresborough Castle, that it was said that Robert of Knaresborough was one of three most popular saints in Europe.

## St Sampson's, Church Street

In 1847 Alfred Hargrove described the churchyard as follows in his *The Baneful Custom of Interment in Towns*: 'as is well known [it] adjoins the fish market. It contains about thirty perches and is in such a disgusting state, that no interments can take place without interfering with human remains ... it is so wet and swampy that graves have been known to be partly filled with water ... and when the coffin has been lowered, it has plunged out of sight into a mass of loathsome mire whilst the mourners have shuddered around'.

## St Sampson's Square

Or Brown's Corner. The square was a slave market in late **Roman** times. Browns was founded by Henry Rhodes Brown in 1891 and has been here since 1900. Davygate nearby is named after David le Lardiner (clerk of the kitchen). His job was to stock the King's larder; in the twelfth century David's father, John,was the Royal lardiner for the Forest of Galtres – a title which became hereditary – David received land from King Stephen in 1135. Davygate was also the site of the forest courthouse prison – the

*Left:* St Sampson's Square – the fine Market Cross which once stood here, demolished in 1815 – from a copper plate originally published in Drake's *The History and Antiquities of the City of York Vol II*, 1785.

*Below:* St Sampson's Square in the 1930s.

only one in the land for incarcerating transgressors of forest laws. During the Civil War Cromwell's army 'shot well nigh forty Hot Fiery bullets' into the square, one of which 'slewe a maide'. The square was the venue for the Thursday hardware market and boasted a fine market cross until its demolition in the 1830s. Plays were staged here. The sign on *The Three Cranes* pub in the square is designed to mislead: the pub is named after the lifting gear used by stallholders rather than anything ornithological.

## St Thomas's Hospital

Next to **Micklegate Bar** but demolished in 1862. In 1851 it was an **almshouse** 'for aged widows' taking in permanent residents and travellers for food and lodging. Until 1791 these widows had to beg on the streets for four days every year for their alms. The Punch Bowl stands on the site now, indicative, like the pub of the same name in Stonegate, of the vogue for drinking punch from the end of the seventeenth century. As a new, fashionable drink it caught on amongst the Whigs leading to the sign of the punchbowl denoting inns patronised by Whigs.

## St William

Archbishop William Fitzherbert, nephew of William the Conqueror and **Archbishop of York** from 1141, was disgraced, vilified by St Bernard ('since many are called and few are chosen') and sacked in 1148 but reinstated on appeal by Pope Anastasius IV. William's embalmed head (he died in suspicious circumstances in 1154 while taking Mass in the

St William's College, 1904.

Minster – a poisoned chalice?) is preserved in **York Minster**. His sainthood derives as much from the fact that the Dean, with one eye on the lucrative pilgrim industry, badly wanted a saint for York to compete with Canterbury's Thomas Becket. In 1227 the Pope made William a saint, acknowledging no doubt William's reputation for miracles – mending broken legs and restoring sight, and the fragrant oils which exuded from his tomb.

### St William's College, College Street

Originally the House of the Prior of Hexham it is named after Archbishop William Fitzherbert (**St William**) and built in 1465 by order of Warwick the Kingmaker. From about 1890 the fifteenth-century half timbering was covered in stucco; it was removed again in 1906. The college was split into tenements at the time but formerly was home to the **Minster's** Chantry: twenty-three priests and their provost. The priests, in **Bedern**, had been indulging in 'colourful nocturnal habits' and were re-billeted in the nearby college so that their behaviour could be monitored more closely. One incident involved one of the cathedral freelances hitting a man over the head with the blunt end of an axe. Charles I established his propaganda **Royal printing house** here during the Civil War and it was used as the **Royal Mint** at one time. The current central doors were made by Robert Thompson of Kilburn: his trademark mouse can be seen on the right hand door. A rental document of 1845 tells us that annual rents are 32s for five tenements, three cottages (2s each) and one messuage (2s 4d). From 1680-1761 the cottages were variously occupied by a painter, joiner, translator, cordwainer. They were nearly demolished in 1912 to make way for the tramline to Heworth. Frank Green, owner of the nearby Treasurer's House, bought the College and gave it in 1906 to the Convocation of York, whose meeting place it was until the amalgamation of the Convocations of York and Canterbury created the Synod of the Church of England. Appropriately, the College now houses the Minster's Visitor Centre, a brass rubbing centre and restaurant. **George Hudson** had a draper's store in one of the shops here.

### Stonegate

By common consent one of the finest streets in England, if not Europe, and York's first 'foot-street', pedestrianised in 1971 and paving the way for many more. You can still see the gallows sign of the Olde Starre Inne stretching across the street. Stonegate was once famous for its coffee shops (hence Coffee Yard). The old **Roman** stone paving – hence the name – survives under the cobbles complete with the central gulley for the chariots' skid wheels. It was the Roman *Via Praetoria*. Queen Mary, wife of George V, when living at Goldsborough Hall near Knaresborough, was a frequent shopper here in the 1920s and '30s: unfortunately for the shop owners she was a devotee of 'honouring' – the practice whereby patronage alone was considered sufficient payment for the goods she left the shops with.

### Stonewall Jackson

Thomas Jonathan 'Stonewall' Jackson (d. 1863) , Confederate General in the American Civil War, visited York in the 1830s. *The Times* reported in his obituary: 'He dwelt with great animation upon the vibration of the air produced by the deep notes of the organ

Stonegate around 1920.

in York Minster ... it is rare to find in a Presbyterian such appreciation and admiration of Cathedral magnificence'.

## The Strays of York

Owned and managed by the Freemen of the city who had grazing rights on their local stray. Pasture Managers looked after each stray, assisted by Herdsman who lived in the cottages on each of the strays: Micklegate, Bootham, Monk and Walmgate.

## The Sweet History of York

A visitor attraction celebrating the city's confectionery heritage opened in King's Square in 2012. It allows visitors to see at first hand the story of York's confectionery industry, past, present and future with a strong emphasis on hands-on activities, anecdotes and memories from former employees of **Rowntree**, **Terry** and **Craven** – and visitors can have a try at making their own chocolate.

## The Temperance Society

The York Temperance Society was set up in 1830 with forty subscribers and **Joseph Rowntree** as Secretary; membership grew to nearly 1,000 by 1936 – 3.3 per cent of the city population at this time . From 1836 there were rival organisations advocating total abstinence and variously called New Temperance, Total Abstinence or Teetotal; an Association of Abstainers started in 1874. The York Temperance Society protested on such issues as the extension of licensing hours to 11.00 p.m., Sunday closing, banning the sale of alcohol to children, and grocers' licences. They were also instrumental in thwarting license renewals at *The Golden Slipper Inn* and *The Corporation Arms* in Friargate. **In Walmgate** alone there were twenty inns, according to *White's 1830 Trade Directory*, so it was nothing if not an upward battle; across the city there was an inn for every twenty-eight families. In the 1890s Joseph Rowntree and Arthur Sherwell published *The Temperance Problem and Social Reform,* although in 1874 records show that Rowntree may not have favoured total abstinence if an order for a case of champagne sent to his home was anything to go by. The book was a bestseller and went on to sell 90,000 copies in nine editions. In 1841 a *Temperance Coffee House* had opened in Colliergate changing to *The Commercial Temperance Hotel* on its move to Low Ousegate in 1843. In 1877 the Society bought a lecture theatre in Goodramgate and renamed it the Victoria Hall. In the early 1890s there was a Temperance Society coffee stand in Queen Street dissuading railway workers from mixing work with drink. In 1929 there were three temperance hotels in York: *The Minster Commercial* in St Martin's Crescent off Micklegate; *Frank's* at 134 Micklegate and *Young's Private & Commercial* at 24 High Petergate. The Temperance Society was set up in Bradford in 1831. Education for all was their mission. A contemporary pamphlet urges residents to 'come as you are, do not stoop to black your boots'.

## Terry, Joseph

Joseph Terry started making cocoa and chocolate in 1886 and had become the market leader of chocolate assortments by the end of the 1920s. Joseph came to York

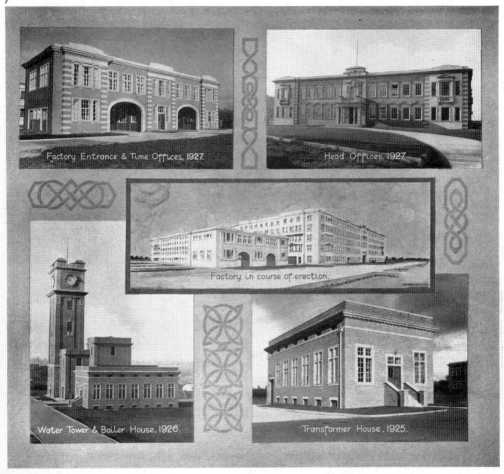

# JOSEPH TERRY & SONS LTD.

Factory Entrance & Time Offices, 1927.

Head Offices, 1927.

Factory in course of erection.

Water Tower & Boiler House, 1926.

Transformer House, 1925.

VIEWS *of* TERRY'S CHOCOLATE WORKS *at* BISHOPTHORPE ROAD

## YORK, ENGLAND

*MANUFACTURERS of*
*Chocolates, Boiled Sugars, Sugared*
*Almonds, Marzipan & Calves' Jelly*

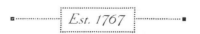
*Est. 1767*

Joseph Terry & Sons Ltd – a 1928 advertisement published in *York Historic Pictorial*.

from nearby Pocklington to serve an apprenticeship in apothecary in **Stonegate**. An advertisement in the *York Courant* in 1813 tells us that he is established 'opposite the Castle, selling spices, pickling vinegar, essence of spruce, patent medicines and perfumery' – the usual stock in trade for an apothecary. Later, he moved this chemist's shop to **Walmgate** . In 1823 he married Harriet Atkinson who was related to Robert Berry; he ran a small confectionery business with William Bayldon near Bootham Bar. Joseph then gave up apothecary and joined Berry in St Helen's Square. George Berry succeeded his father to form Terry & Berry but George left in 1826 leaving Joseph to develop the confectionery business. Joseph Terry was Governor of the **Merchant Adventurers** in 1881, **Lord Mayor** three times and was knighted in 1897.

## Terry's of York

Terry's moved to their purpose-built Baroque Revival building in 1930 from the Clementhorpe site which they had occupied since 1862. By 1840 Terry's products were being delivered to seventy-five towns all over England; products included candied eringo, coltfoot rock, gumballs and lozenges made from squill, camphor and horehound. Apart from boiled sweets they also made marmalade, marzipan, mushroom ketchup and calves' jelly. Conversation lozenges, precursors of *Love Hearts* (with such slogans as 'Can you polka?', 'I want a wife', 'Do you love me?' and 'How do you flirt?'), were particularly popular. Chocolate production began around 1867 with thirteen chocolate products adding to the other 380 or so confectionery and parfait lines. Before the Second World War 'Theatre Chocolates' were available with rustle-proof wrappers. The famous *Chocolate Orange* (which started life as a *Chocolate Apple*) was born in 1932 and at one point one in ten Christmas stockings reputedly contained a *Terry's Chocolate Orange*. In the 1990s seven million boxes of *All Gold* were sold in a year.

## Terry's Restaurant

In St Helen's Square. The first floor cafe-restaurant and ballroom and ground floor shop were as famous in their time as **Bettys** (directly opposite in the square) is now. Items on the menu in 1900 included: Russian tea (6d); Scotch Woodcock (1s); Harum Scarum (2s) and Gentleman's Relish Sandwich (1s). In 1924 **Harker's Hotel** (then opposite) opposed the renewal of Terry's music licence on the grounds that the music and dancing were keeping guests awake and making the owner ill. Terry's counsel submitted at one point that 'jazz might not be music but a very large number of people like it'. The licence was renewed on condition that Terry's kept the windows closed. The restaurant closed in 1980 although the Terry's name lives on between the Corinthian pillars. The wood panelling still survives inside and came to Terry's as a result of a cancelled order from a ocean going liner. Apart from their prestigious St Helen's Square restaurant, outside catering was big business for Terry's with functions catering for Bird's Eye in the **Assembly Rooms**, the **Lord Mayor's** parties in nearby **Mansion House** and dinners at the **Merchant Taylor's Hall**. Queen Elizabeth was entertained twice and the Duke of Kent once at the Mansion House. One early 1960s Assembly Room lunch

Terry's Restaurant – a 1930s advertisement for this prestigious establishment

involved 380 vegetarian meals, including food for ten vegans – all very new then. Hunt balls and army functions for officers and wives from Catterick were frequent and at one Tadcaster Hunt Ball the guests reputedly included Christine Keeler, Mandy Rice Davies and John Profumo.

## Theatre Royal

The first theatre was built nearby on tennis courts in Minster Yard in 1734 by Thomas Keregan. In 1744 his widow built The New Theatre here on what was the city's **Mint**, itself built on the site of **St Leonard's Hospital**. In 1765 it was rebuilt by Joseph Baker and enlarged to seat 550, 'by far the most spacious in Great Britain, Drury Lane and Covent garden excepted', according to the *York Courant*. Access to the site of the Mint can still be gained from the back of the main stage. At this time the theatre was illegal and it was not until a Royal Patent was granted in 1769 and the theatre was renamed the Theatre Royal that this status changed. Gas lighting came in 1824 and in 1835 a new frontage was built facing onto the newly-created St Leonard's Place. This was removed to Fulford Road in 1880 and replaced with a new facade.

York Theatre Royal: a scene from
*The Desert Song* in 1957.

## Thomas's Hotel, Museum Street

Dates from around 1700. The doorway boasts a colourful relief sculpture depicting a court jester with bauble and a well-dressed Sir Walter Raleigh type figure with tankard and pipe. What does it tell us? That this is the place to come for a drink, a smoke and a good laugh.

## The Three Legged Mare

This pub is named after a triangular type of industrial gallows which despatched three felons at once; one was in use at the **Knavesmire** until 1801 before it was removed in 1812. There is a replica of the 'wonkey donkey' in the beer garden of the pub in Low Petergate. There is no future in riding the three-legged mare.

## The RMS *Titanic*

The *Titanic* claimed the lives of two York men when it sank in 1912: J. Foley, forty-four-year-old storekeeper, and C. Stagg, thirty-seven-year-old steward.

## Toft Green

Once a military parade and training ground used for displays of arms, mock battles, and the construction of military engines – all for the defence of the city; the green was also the site of horse and cattle fairs and a **House of Correction**. From 1700 Lady Hewley's **almshouse** hospital was here. It earned the name Pageant Green as it was the starting point for the **Mystery Plays**.

## Trade & Industry

York, because of its cloth trade and the ancillary industries associated with it in the fourteenth century, was described as 'the foremost industrial town in the North of England.' In 1384 there were 800 weavers in the city. This was short-lived though, and the trade in cloth declined to such a degree that a visitor to the city in the seventeenth century, Thomas Fuller, remarked: 'the foreign trade is like their river ... low and flat.' **Francis Drake** records in his *Eboracum: or the History and Antiquities of the City of York*, that York in the eighteenth century had precious little industry and the only real commercial activity was butter exports, corn and wine trading. **Daniel Defoe**, in *A Tour Through the Whole Island of Great Britain* at first disagrees, describing 'considerable trade' with France, Norway and Portugal, and then, in contradiction, agrees: 'here is no trade ... except such as depends upon the confluence of the gentry.' This industrial lethargy was due to some extent both to the high price of coal which had to be shipped from the coalfields of the West Riding, and to the restrictive, exclusive attitude of the local **Merchant Adventurers** and their insistence that all traders had to be **Freemen** of the City up until 1827. The **railway** and **confectionery** industries were soon to change the industrial landscape.

## Trams

The laying of electric tramlines in 1910 replaced the horse drawn trams. In 1900 there had been eleven such trams drawn by horses from a pool of thirty-three. The tramlines

A tram lit up for George VI's Coronation in 1911.

'York's New Electric Tramcars, January 1910.'

were all taken up again in 1935 as car use increased. The last journey from Nessgate on 16 November was witnessed by large crowds gathered at midnight to watch the **Lord Mayor** and Inspector J. Stewart – the driver of the very first service – drive York trams into oblivion. The electrification cost £89,741; over 8 miles of track were laid. The first day of the tram service, 20 January 1910, saw 6,786 passengers carried with fares totalling £35 18s 5d – as the fare was 2d there must have been quite a few fare dodgers. Rail cars (as trams were called) plied between Fulford and South Bank; Fulford and Acomb; Haxby Road and South Bank and Haxby Road and Acomb – and vice versa on a ten minute service between 8.00 a.m. and 10.45, plus works specials; 2-10 on Sundays. The universal fare was 2d (less than 1p) per journey.

## Treasurer's House

A magnificent building in Minster Yard on the site of a building once used by the Treasurer to the Minster until 1547. Radolphus was the first Treasurer in 1100; his special house was built on the site of the Roman garrison and was probably razed to the ground in the great fire of 1137. The present building combines a rebuild from around 1300 and a Grade 1 listed Jacobean town house with distinctive Flemish gables. Each room is laid out in the style of a different period, as instructed by Frank Green who donated it complete with contents to the National Trust. The Parliamentarian general Sir Thomas Fairfax, of Marston Moor fame, once owned it; by the nineteenth century,

William and Mary's Staircase, Treasurer's House.

though it was reduced to a 'a bug-ridden slum'. A **Roman** street, the Via Decumana, was excavated under the cellar in the 1960s, substantiating stories about ghostly legionaries.

## Tuke, Mary

Mary Tuke was descended from a famous Quaker family; her grandfather was jailed for non-conformism in the 1660s. In 1725, age thirty, Mary established a grocery business, first in **Walmgate,** then **Castlegate**, and, after a number of legal wrangles with **York Merchant Adventurers Company**, finally won the right to trade as a grocer in 1732. The relevant, curious Latin-cum-English inscription on the *Freeman's Roll of the City of York* reads: 'Maria Tuke, spinster Fil Willelmi Tuke, blacksmith.'

## Tuke, William

Mary Tuke was joined by her nephew William in 1746 as an apprentice; he inherited the business on her death in 1752 and became a freeman grocer and member of the **Merchant Adventurers**. The shop specialised in the sale of coffee, chicory and drinking chocolate; his son Henry, at that time halfway through a medical degree, gave it all up in 1785 in a typically Quakerish act and joined the business. They branched out to sell tea (the firm was later taken over by Twinings) and to manufacture cocoa and chocolate themselves. Brands such *Tukes' Rich Cocoa, Tukes' Plain Chocolate, British Cocoa Coffee* and *Tukes' Milk Chocolate* (not milk chocolate as we know it but

Dick Turpin swaggers into York before his appointment at Tyburn – as reconstructed in the 1971 Pageant of York.

chocolate used for mixing with milk) were brought to market. William Tuke set up the ground breaking, influential psychiatric hospital, the **Retreat**, in 1796.

## Turpin, Dick

Highwayman Dick Turpin, also known as John Palmer, was hanged (somewhat fittingly) on the Knavesmire in 1739, for horse stealing – 'a crime worthy of death'. Turpin spent his last six months in the Debtors' Prison, which was built in 1701-5 and is now part of the **Castle Museum**; the other half of the museum was originally the Female Prison, built in 1780-83. The museum, which opened in 1938, is named after York **Castle**, which originally stood on the site. Turpin had many visitors: his jailer is said to have earned £100 from selling drinks to Turpin and his guests; Turpin bought a new frock coat and shoes and hired five mourners for £3 10s for the occasion. A report in *The Gentleman's Magazine* for 7 April 1739 notes Turpin's arrogance: 'Turpin behaved in an undaunted manner; as he mounted the ladder, feeling his right leg tremble, he spoke a few words to the topsman, then threw himself off, and expir'd in five minutes'. The short drop method of hanging meant that those executed were killed by slow strangulation: Turpin was left hanging until late afternoon, before being cut down and taken to *The Blue Boar Inn* in **Castlegate**. Turpin's grave in St George's churchyard was dug particularly deep to deter **body snatchers**; to no avail: the corpse was removed and found later at the back of **Stonegate** in a surgeon's garden. Before reburial the coffin was filled with lime. Black Bess, Turpin's steed, was an elaboration added later by writers such as William Harrison Ainsworth in *Rockwood* (1878) and Eliza Cook in her *Black Bess* (1869), an interesting line from which reads: 'And the fame of Dick Turpin had been something less If he'd ne'er rode to York on his bonnie Black Bess'.

## Tyburn

York's Tyburn gallows had been on the **Knavesmire** from 1379; public **executions** became a popular part of a day at the races. The last hanging was in 1801 – Edward Hughes was the convict, guilty of rape – after which the gallows were moved to the **New Drop** near the castle. A paved area with a small plaque today marks where the scaffold was – on Tadcaster Road, opposite Pulleyn Drive. It was originally a gibbet post; the gallows replaced the gibbet in 1379 and remained until finally pulled down in 1812. Other gallows existed in **Burton Stone Lane** controlled by the abbot of **St Mary's Abbey** and at the Horse Fair, at the junction of the Haxby and Wiggington Roads. There were gallows on Foss Bridge administered by the **Archbishop of York.** Those owned by St Leonard's church were on Green Dykes, now Garrow Hill and close to Thief Lane along which convicted robbers were led to the scaffold.

## Unitarian Chapel

Built in 1693 in St Saviourgate four years after the Act of Toleration legalised non-conformist places of worship. Originally built for Presbyterians by Lady Sarah Hewley it is, unusually, in the shape of a Greek cross.

## University of York

The first petition for a university in York was to King James I in 1617 followed by other unsuccessful attempts in the eighteenth century, one to annex it to the existing **medical school.** In 1903 F. J. Munby and others (including the **Yorkshire Philosophical Society**) proposed a 'Victoria University of Yorkshire'. What was then the **College of Ripon and York St John** considered purchasing **Heslington Hall** as part of a proposed new campus. The campus lake is the largest plastic-bottomed lake in Europe and attracts many waterfowl; the campus also supports a large rabbit population, the hunting of which by students is strictly prohibited. Heslington Hall is a fine Elizabethan manor built by Thomas Eymes in 1568; Eymes was secretary to Henry VIII's Great Council of the North which had its headquarters in **King's Manor**; as with other buildings of the time, it was constructed in the shape of an 'E', in honour of Queen Elizabeth I.

## Vanbrugh, Sir John

Sir John, dramatist and architect of Blenheim Palace and Castle Howard, married Henrietta Maria Yarburgh of Heslington Hall in St Lawrence's Church on 14 January 1719. St Lawrence was rebuilt in 1883 and is the city's largest parish church.

## Vavasours

Catholic family who owned Peter's Post Quarry near Tadcaster where stone for the **Minster** was quarried. They owned Hazlewood Castle where they were given special privileges by Elizabeth I to celebrate mass, in return for providing the stone. Ann Vavasour was a favourite maid of honour of Elizabeth's and the mysterious 'dark lady' of Shakespeare's *Sonnets*. A statue of William Vavasour stands at the west door of the Minster holding a block of stone destined for the Minster. Dorothy Vavasour, a friend of **Margaret Clitherow's**, died for her faith in **Kidcotes** in 1587.

## Vianomenology

Another neologism. York has some delightful, and fascinating street and **snickelway** names. It is the only city where gates are streets and bars are gates. Here is a random selection and their, sometimes putative, derivations and histories:

*Aldwark* = old works, walls.

*Bedern* – named after the chapel – a place of bidding.

*Blake Street* – either from bleke, white paved road, or from the Norse bleg, indicating the Viking leather trade and bleaching.

*Blossom Street*, formerly Ploxamgate, Ployhsuaingate and Ploxswaingate – street of the ploughmen.

*Bootham* – street of the market stall holders.

*Brownie Dyke* (on the Foss close to Castle Mills) = brun eau dyke – brown water dyke.

*Buckingham Street* – named after George Villers, 'butcher' Duke of Buckingham; see **Executions**.

*Carr's Lane* – after **John Carr**.

*Church Street*, originally Girdlergate, girdle-makers' street.

*Coffee Yard*, took this name (after Langton Lane) when the coffee houses started to spring up.

*College Street*, formerly Little Alice Lane and then Vicar Lane – the vicars speak for themselves, not so little Alice; she was possibly an old lady who ran an alehouse there in the 1730s.

*Collier Street* – after the charcoal burners.

*Coney Street*: King Street but also Cunny Street in 1622.

*Coppergate* – nothing to do with copper or cooper, but rather street of the joiners or turners.

*Cromwell Road* – after Oliver; previously Gaol Lane, after the jail in **Bitchdaughter Tower**.

*Davygate* – named after David le Lardiner – clerk of the royal kitchen.

*Elbow Lane* – describes its crookedness.

*Fairfax Street*, named after Thomas, Lord Fairfax, the Parliamentarian general whose house was in Skeldergate.

*Feasegate* – Norse for cowhouse street.

*Fetter Lane* – Feltergayle, felt workers' street.

*Footless Lane*: possibly a reference to the disabilities of some of the patients at nearby **St Leonard's Hospital**; later Museum Street (qv).

*Grape Lane* – a place for a grope.

*Hornpot Lane* – where the horn and comb breakers worked.

**Hungate**, originally Hundegat in Mersch = Dog Street in the Bog, formerly
    Dunnyngdykes = Dung Dump.

*Jewbury* or Jew's burh, where the Jews lived.

*Jubbergate* – Brettgate in the twelfth century after the Bretons who lived here (see also
    Navigation Road); Joubrettgate in 1280 when the Jews moved in.

*King Street*; once Kergate meaning muddy street.

**Lady Peckett's Yard** – after Lady Mayoress Alice Peckett; formerly Bacusgail or Back
    House Lane, and Trichourgail – street of the tricksters.

*Layerthorpe* – hamlet where the deer congregate; a reference to the Forest of Galtres
    on the edge of the city.

*Lendal* – formerly Aldeconyngstrete or Old Coney Street. Lendal is a contraction
    of Landing Hill – a reference to St Leonard's Landing, a staithe or landing on the
    **Ouse** used to import stone for the building of the **Minster**.

*Lord Mayor's Walk* – formerly Goose Lane; opened in 1718 in a grand ceremony to
    mark its elegance.

**Mad Alice Lane**, named after Alice Smith, a resident hanged for the crime of insanity
    in 1825.

**Micklegate**: Great Street; originally Myglagata.

*Minster Gates* – formerly Bookland Lane and Book-binders Lane in the sixteenth
    century.

**Mucky Peg Lane** – named after a resident of ill repute; other etymologies derive from
    Pig rather than Peg.

*Museum Street* – in the thirteenth century Ffotelsgate or Footless Lane (qv); then
    Finkle Street and in the seventeenth century Back Lendal and Little Lendal in 1782.

*Navigation Road* – after the Foss Navigation; in the thirteenth century it was Little
    Brettgate – another street of the Bretons, French traders.

*North Street*: Nordstreta, one of the few streets to have retained the Anglo Saxon
    strete rather than adopting the Norse gata or gayle.

*Nunnery Lane* after the convent, once Beggargate.

*Ogleforth* – simply Ugel's place.

*Parliament Street* – after the Act of Parliament of 1833 which allowed for the market
    here.

**Pavement** – **Domesday** has it as Marketshyre; later renamed on account it was a rare
    piece of paved land in the city.

*Peasholme Green* – place where peas were grown; later the site of the wool market.

*Piccadilly* – created in 1840 and named after Piccadilly in London.

*Pope's Head Alley* – a reference to a papal effigy here?

**Shambles**, originally in Macello – the first of many names described above.

*Silver Street* – after the fish in the fish market.

*Skeldergate* – from the Norse skjaldari, Shield Makers Street.

*Spen Lane*, once Ispyn Lane and Isping Giel referring to the aspens growing here;

*Spurriergate*: street of the spur makers.

*St Maurice's Road*; once Barker Hill – street of tanners and parchment makers – both
   used bark to make tannin; in 1340 the ramparts here were called Herlot Hill
   after the local beggars. By the eighteenth century it was Love Lane or Harlot Hill
   denoting it as a denizen of prostitutes.

*St Saviourgate* – formerly Ketmongergate or flesh seller street.

*Stonebow* – stone arch, possibly Roman; once Whitefriar Lane after the Carmelite
   friary here.

**Stonegate** refers to the Roman Porta Praetoria, a gate into the Roman garrison.

*Swinegate*; originally Patrick Pool then Swyngaill after the pig houses and the 1605
   pig market.

*Tanner Row* and *Tanner's Moat* – signified the tanneries located around here

*Thief Lane*, the road along which convicted robbers were led to the scaffold at
   Garrow Hill.

*Tower Street* – originally Castlegate Postern Lane after Castlegate Postern since
   demolished; site of the ducking stool.

*Victor Street* after Victoria Bar in 1838; once St Mary's Road after the church and
   Lounelithgate: hidden gateway.

**Whipmawhopmagate**: call that a street!

What is also quite remarkable is the mix of languages represented: Latin, Anglo Saxon,
Norse, Early English, Early German, Norman French – all tracking the city's history
over time.

### Queen Victoria

In 1854 Victoria, Albert and five of their children stopped off at York for a short while
on the way to Balmoral. There was some local opposition to the cost of such a short
visit, and Victoria got wind of it. So unamused was she that she never visited the city
again in the remaining forty-seven years of her reign.

### Victoria Bar

This bar was built in 1838 and named after the new **Queen**. It gave access to the
city in the Nunnery Lane area. During construction an earlier archway was
uncovered which showed signs of having been hastily blocked up. This was probably
the twelfth century bar known as Lounelith, or 'secluded gate'; the blockade was
possibly part of the strengthening of the city's defences in the Northern Rebellion in
1569.

### The Walker Iron Foundry

Founded in 1837 by John Walker (1801-1853) 'Iron & brass founder, bell-hanger &
smith', in Dixon's Yard, **Walmgate**. They provided the first gas lamps and railings for
St Leonards Place, the gates at Dean's Park and the surrounding railings and gas lights.
In 1845-46 Walker supplied the gates to Kew Gardens, a commission which earned
them the patronage of Queen Victoria in 1847 when she granted them permission
to describe themselves as 'Ironfounders & Purveyors of Smithy Work to the Queen'.

Walmgate: Hill's Yard about 1906.

In 1853 they supplied the ten ton gates and railings to the British Museum. London. Other commissions included gates at Sandringham, the Botanical Gardens in Mauritius and the palace of the Maharajah Holkar of India. Renamed Thomlinson-Walker the firm moved to the Victoria Foundry at 76 **Walmgate.**

## Walmgate

This was a place of great poverty, crime, alcohol-related violence and prostitution, like **Hungate**, for many years. The infant mortality rate was one in three before age one – as highlighted by **Seebohm Rowntree's** ground-breaking *Poverty: A Study in Town Life* in 1901 for which researchers visited 11,500 families and found that twenty-five per cent of the city population was visibly poor – in *'obvious want and squalor'*. The pungent smell of hide, skins and fat from local industries added to the horror of the place. At the end of the 1880s there were 8,000 midden privies in York, many here and in Hungate. In Walmgate in 1913, the death rate was twenty-three per 1,000, almost twice York's average. Using powers under the 1930 Housing Act, York Corporation began to clear the slums: streets off Walmgate and in Hungate were demolished, and residents moved to new estates outside the city centre.

## Walmgate Bar

Originally known as Walbesgate this is the only York Bar with its barbican intact, thanks largely to **William Etty RA** who campaigned tirelessly for its preservation. In 1489 it was set on fire by rebels and then bombarded in the Civil War. The inner facade is sixteenth century and still retains its Doric and Ionic columns.

## The Wapentake of Ainsty

A Wapentake is a subdivision of a county. The Wapentake of Ainsty, taking in thirty-five townships, lay largely to the west of the city of York between the Rivers Ouse, Wharfe and Nidd and was named after Ainsty Cliff near Bilborough which in turn is named after the **Roman** road which ran nearby.

## Ward, Mary

Mary Ward (d. 1645) is celebrated in the museum that is an integral part of the **Bar Convent**. She is buried in St Thomas's in **Osbaldwick**. She founded the Institute of the Blessed Virgin Mary opening schools in Flanders before it was suppressed by the Pope. After imprisonment in Munich for heresy she returned to England and re-established the Institute in Heworth in 1644. The fifty pictures on the Bar Convent staircase depict her life; they are reproduced from seventeenth century paintings from the house of the Institute of Augsburg. The 2,000 or so books in the library date from between 1508 and 1850 and, unlike some library collections, are well used, obviously read, and annotated. The convent also retains a relic of the hand of St **Margaret Clitherow**. In 1977 the day school and boarding school here merged to become the Bar Convent Grammar School when boys were admitted for the first time; in 1985 it became part of All Saints' Catholic School.

## Whip-Ma-Whop-Ma-Gate

At thirty-five yards in length this is the city's smallest surviving street between **Pavement** and Colliergate. Much speculation surrounds the meaning of the name which was once Whitnourwhatnourgate; it is probably more an expression of incredulity than anything else: something like: 'A street? Call that a street!' There is a door with the number 28½ here.

## White, John and Grace

**Stonegate** printer 'over against the Star' and the only one in the country brave enough to take on the **printing** of William of Orange's manifesto after his landing at Torbay in 1688. White was imprisoned at Hull for his troubles until the city surrendered to William. The king promptly rewarded him with a warrant appointing him 'Their Majesties' Printer for the City of York and the Five Northern Counties'. His widow, Grace, was the first woman to establish a newspaper here in 1718, *The York Mercury*, in Coffee Yard.

## White Rose Dairy, New Earswick

The inspiration of **Seebohm Rowntree**; he established the dairy to ensure the provision of clean milk to village residents in the knowledge that contaminated milk was a factor in high infant mortality rates. To do this he brought in a Dane, Wilfred Sorensen (known locally and geographically inaccurately as Oslo), from the Manchester Pure Milk Co, bought some land for him to build a farm on and on which to develop a herd. Unusually for the time high levels of hygiene were adopted: the milk was filtered and cooled to destroy bacteria.

## Whittock, Nathaniel (b. 1791)

The artist who drew the stunning lithograph which depicts in amazing detail the buildings of York from a position in the south-west a few hundred feet above Blossom Street. Advertisements in the *Yorkshire Gazette* in 1856 list the numerous points of interest 'the beautiful original drawing ... embracing every object of interest in the City and Environs ... even the lamp-posts have not escaped the keen observation of the artist'. A must see.

## William of Malmesbury

Writing in 1125 the father of British history shows us how little has really changed with regard to the north-south divide: 'Next in rank after Canterbury is York ... almost everything about the language of the North, and particularly of the people of York, is so crude and discordant that we southerners cannot understand it. This is because they are near to barbarian peoples [the Scots] and far from the English kings'.

## The Workhouse

In 1551, part of **St Anthony's Hall**, one of **York's Houses of Correction** at the time, was used for use as a poorhouse. In 1567 and 1569, two weaving establishments were established for the unemployed in St Anthony's Hall and St George's House, but the goods they produced were useless. After many unsuccessful attempts a number of the city's parishes set up a joint workhouse in 1768 to accommodate ninety paupers in a former cotton factory at 26 Marygate, again, working with textiles. York Poor Law Union was established in 1837 and took over Marygate: hygiene left much to be desired, according to this 1839 inspection, after an outbreak of food poisoning from a vat of soup: 'In a room, however, in my opinion as a Chemist, ill adapted for the purpose of preserving meat, we found a Beast's Head at that time offensive to the smell ... This room adjoins and opens into a short and very narrow yard considerably tainted with all the effluvia rising from some privies at one end ... The head not having been previously cleaned, a quantity of unwholesome mucus was attached to it.' The Guardians nevertheless concluded that the soup had made inmates ill because 'the usual quantity of Potatos [*sic*] had been omitted making the soup too strong and rich'. The Poor Law Commissioners recommended a replacement for the Marygate workhouse reporting 'a permanent reservoir of foul air'; and the privies were 'without exception in an offensive state'. Most of the inmates were 'children, the aged and infirm and persons of weak mind'; many, if not all, were diseased and children mixed 'in the infectious wards with adults labouring under syphilis and gonorrhea'. The paupers mocked the idiots 'as a pastime'. In August 1845, the *Leeds Mercury* reported on the women's ward in an official inspection: 'this place is used by aged idiots, women and children, and besides being of limited extent, it has only one privy, with an open cesspool'. In 1849 a new union workhouse was built on Huntington Road housing 300 inmates. Different inmates were separated by a network of walls, including one specifically for unmarried women and one for 'female idiots'. There was also a washhouse, laundry, and the mortuary. On the men's side were an oakum-picking shop, carpenter's shop, stone yard, and a coach-house. In 1930, the workhouse became a Public Assistance Institution, while part of the building became of York City Hospital. In 1946, it was renamed the Grange, and in 1955 became St Mary's Hospital. This closed in the late 1970s and the buildings were converted to student accommodation.

## World War I York

Castle Yard became an internment camp for aliens, as did a field in Leeman Road. The **Cattle Market** was a horse depot. The military requisitioned the **de Grey Rooms,** the Exhibition Hall and the Railway Institute; **Knavesmire** was a drill ground; an aerodrome was built at Copmanthorpe; 700 Belgian refugees were lodged in private houses; a canteen for travelling troops opened on **York Railway Station;** VAD hospitals opened in **Clifford Street** and at **St John's College;** stranded soldiers were given supper, bed and breakfast in **the Assembly Rooms** – 435 in one record night with over 100,000 all told.

## Wormald Cut

On the **River Foss** and named after Samuel Wormald, owner of a brewery and timber yard here and presumably one of the financiers of the scheme.

## Xaveria, Sister Mary

Born in 1784 Sister Mary was a nun and a teacher at the **Bar Convent** and became Headmistress at the Poor School there in 1830. An earlier appointment was at St George's School in Walmgate where she taught 'a disorderly crowd of wild-looking little creatures for the most part barefooted, squalid and dirty, shouting and screaming'. Her solution was, in uncanny anticipation of Sister Maria in *The Sound of Music,* to sing and her voice 'acted like magic on the undisciplined audience. In a few moments they were standing silent and almost motionless'.

## Yellow Mixture

Patented by Charles Croskell (d. 1891) who ran his pharmacy in **Parliament Street** selling copious amounts of the famous eponymous *Yellow Mixture*, highly efficacious in teething babies and for other infant ailments. His *Female Pills* were the best remedy for every female disease: heart palpitations, pains in the side and breasts, headache, sallow complexion, depression of spirits, feebleness and swelling of the limbs.

## The York Arms

In High **Petergate** on the site of the **Peter Prison**. In 1818 it was *The Chapter Coffee House* then *The Eclipse, The Board* after an 1838 rebuild back to *The Chapter Coffee House* in 1843 and *The York Arms* in 1860.

## York Assay Office

A sign of York's importance in mediaeval times is that under a 1423 Act the city was the first outside London to receive a touch mark to guarantee the quality of gold and silver sold from the **Mint** here. In 1560 the Corporation decreed that all work in these metals must be 'towched with the pownce of the citie, called halfe leopard head and halfe flower de luyce'; this changed to the Arms of York in 1700. The office closed in 1858.

## York Cats

The hallmark of Tom Adams, the York architect who died in 2006. Black cats on buildings in **Bedern**, King's Square, Walmgate, Gillygate and **Coney Street** indicate his work and are reminiscent of Leonardo da Vinci (who used a cat) rather than Robert Thompson of Kilburn. There are around twenty-three in all (or there were – some have been catnapped) – by Tom Adams and Jonathan Newdick.

## York City Aerodrome

Opened in 1936, five years after Airspeed Ltd was established in York in Piccadilly Bus Garage designing aeroplanes and gliders. The company was run by Neville Shute, later to become a bestselling author. Later, Yorkshire Aviation Services operated from Clifton Moor offering flying lessons and an air taxi service; it became an RAF base during the Second World War.

## York City Library

Originally in Clifford Street, the library in Exhibition Place changed its name in 2010 to the Explore York Learning Centre to reflect a wider range of services and research facilities. The local history collection and archives go back 800 years with over 20,000 books covering the history of York and its surrounding area, as well as local magazines and journals such as the *Yorkshire Archaeological Journal, The Yorkshire Dalesman, Yorkshire Life, the Yorkshire Journal,* and *Thoresby Society Publications.* The earliest newspaper in the collection is the **York Courant** of 1728; from this year up to the present, there is a continuous run of indexed newspapers with titles including the *Yorkshire Gazette, the York Herald, and the Yorkshire Evening Press.* It also keeps maps and plans showing the development of York from the seventeenth century – the earliest map in the collection is John Speed's *Plan of York in 1610.* The Library has poll books for eighteenth and nineteenth century York and Yorkshire and electoral registers for the City of York from 1832 until the present day. York Civic Archives start with the Henry II charter in 1155. The *York Memorandum Book* is the earliest record of Council meetings and provides a unique view of life in fourteenth and fifteenth century York. There is a record of every single meeting of the City Council in a continuous series of *House Books & Minute Books* from 1746. In addition there are over 12,000 architects' and engineers' plans, dating from the 1850s. The Poor Law collection dates from the 1830s to the welfare state in 1948, and contains records of everyone admitted to the York **Workhouse.** Most of the letters to and from York artist **William Etty** are here as are many of the manuscripts of astronomers **John Goodricke** and Edward Pigott.

## York Cocoa House

In Blake Street; this is the city's first dedicated chocolate house since the **Tuke's** establishment in the 1820s. Opened in late 2011 it produces, and serves, chocolate and cocoa on the premises; it is run by the same team as *Little Pretty Things* established in 2009 to provide 'a home for true chocolate lovers'. The core business is regular chocolate making talks and classes, chocolate tasting sessions and workshops illuminating York's chocolate industry heritage, many of which take place in the **Mansion House**.

## York College for Girls

The College was established in 1908 at 62 High Petergate in a fine building that is, in parts, at least 300 years old; it closed in 1997 and is now an Italian Restaurant. The first Headmistress had the nickname E³, derived from her initials – Elizabeth Emma Ellett. Former pupil's include Dame Janet Baker, OBE.

## York Confectionery Company

Founded in 1867 in Fossgate, moving to Fenwick Street off Bishopthorpe Road. It specialised in candied peel and red and white mint rock for the seaside market. York Confectionery Company was owned by a man called Henderson; little is known about him apart from that he suffered from dyspnea, shortness of breath, and his factory became known as Puffy's as a result. He went bankrupt in 1909.

## York Electricity Generating Station

The lights first went on in York in 1899. The ground around the station (run by York Corporation Electricity Committee) vibrated with the noise and the 30000 horse power created by the generating station. The chimney has survived but all else is gone.

## York Fire & Life Insurance Company

Established in 1824 in **St Helen's Square**; its income in 1897 amounted to £223,111 with funds of just over £1 million. It was acquired by General Accident in 1967 and, via Commercial Union and Norwich Union, eventually became part of Aviva in 2009. Today the building is **Harker's** Bar, named after the hotel which stood opposite **Terry's** here before its 1929 demolition and move to Dringhouses.

## York Gas Light Company

Gas lighting, or 'the lamp that wouldn't blow out', was introduced to York by the York Gas Light Company in 1823 on the banks of the **River Foss** near Monk Bridge. In 1836 the York Union Gas Light Company was formed; rivalry was intense with workmen from the former going round filling in the latter's excavations; the two companies eventually amalgamated in 1843 to form the York United Gas Light Company. In 1824 there were 250 consumers; this had risen to 34,000 by 1963. In 1912 coverage was extended to 7 miles from the **Ouse Bridge** to take in Haxby, Wigginton and Strensall.

## York Golf Club

The original club house was built in 1907; York Golf Club was founded in 1890 at the

Knavesmire. The fact that it was on public land caused problems: cows, horses and other livestock grazed on land also frequented by nursemaids with their perambulators. One of the early club rules was indicative of the hazards: 'Members are to refrain from striking while people or cattle are in the way'. An early guide described it as '*apt to be sticky*'. To avoid accidents to man and beast the Club moved to what was army land in Strensall in 1904. The Army has always been important to the Club as illustrated by the fact that the Presidency is always held by the senior officer of the York garrison. A clear-out in the Club in 1960 revealed a large number of oldgolf bags and clubs – some of which had not been collected by soldiers who failed to return from the the First World War.

## York Ham

York ham is a dry- cured ham; according to legend, it obtained its unique flavour from the sawdust from the oak timbers used in the building of **York Minster**. However, York hams have never been smoked although they are distinguished by the fact that the pigs' legs are long cut – they are rounded at the hip rather than squared off. *Law's Grocer's Manual* of 1949 tells us that 'In England the principal ham is long-cut, pale-dried dry-salt cured ham known as York Ham'. Other local regional delicacies include York mayne bread, very popular – by-laws were passed urging people to bake it – up to 1622 when spiced cake stole the market; this may have been in the form of **Ouse Bridge** cakes known in the eighteenth century, a type of Yorkshire tea cake. There was also York Gingerbread, the recipe for which was included in Sarah Martin's 1795 *New Experienced English Housekeeper,* and **Fulford Biscuits.**

## The York-Knaresborough Railway

The 1848 opening of the York to Knaresborough Line by two of the railways which became the North Eastern Railway: the Leeds Northern Railway and the East and West Yorkshire Junction Railway. This line was initially forced to stop at a temporary station at Haya Park because the famous viaduct across the Nidd at Knaresborough collapsed just before being completed in 1848.

## York Medical Society

York Medical Society was founded off **Stonegate** by seven medical men in 1832 for 'the purpose of promoting and diffusing medical knowledge'. This was intended to build on the work of the York Gild of **Barber-Surgeons** which had looked after the training and licensing of medical practitioners, standards of treatment and professional education in the city from the fourteenth century. The minutes of the society provide a fascinating record of rapid changes in medicine, diagnosis, epidemiology and social change, all reflected in the lectures given there over the years. The society was active in driving social change and in improving living conditions: a paper from 1842 entitled 'A Plan of Political Medicine' anticipated the ethos and practicalities of the National Health Service by over 100 years. York's pre-eminence in psychiatric medicine and patient care (as exemplified by the **Retreat**) is reflected in the society's work. There were also close links with York's first **Medical School** which thrived between 1834 and 1858. Indeed, the annual Oration and other lectures were the main source of postgraduate medical education in the city for many years. Much of the timber framed house goes back to 1590 (as evidenced by the dated lead rain-water head over the entrance doors – the oldest surviving in York) although parts such as the wing known as Little Paradise to the left of the entrance and one of the fireplaces are older still. Extensive alterations and additions took place in the seventeenth and eighteenth centuries. A dispensary and consulting rooms were developed and the west wing was added by **Dr Tempest Anderson**; the speaking tube from Dr Anderson's bed to the front door to address night callers can still be seen. Sales of the properties bought by Anderson's family after his death paid for the wing he bequeathed to the **Yorkshire Philosophical Society** at the **Yorkshire Museum**. The Yorkshire Law Society, established in 1786 and the second oldest Law Society in the UK, set up its library here in 1944.

## The York Mercury

*The York Mercury*, York' s earliest newspaper printed by **Grace White**, the owner of her late husband's printing house in Coffee Yard, was published first on 23 February 1719. Its title then was *The York Mercury, or a general View of the Affairs of Europe but more particularly of Great Britain, with useful observations about Trade*. Charles Bourne took over the printing house in 1721 and in 1724 **Thomas Gent**, author of *History of the Famous City of York*, acquired the business. Gent's first issue, for 16-23 November 1724, appeared under the comparatively brief new title *Original York Journal*, or *Weekly Courant*. By 1728 it was *The Original Mercury, York Journal, or Weekly Courant* and was published until 1739.

## York Public Cemetery

Laid out in 1837 to provide better end of life facilities than the city's sporadic, overcrowded parish and non-conformist (Quakers excepted) burial grounds could now offer. The chapel and gatehouse were designed by local architect James Pigott Pritchett based on the Erechtheon on the Acropolis in Athens. Increasing cremations in the post-war years seriously affected the viability of the company and the cemetery fell into serious disrepair. It was eventually salvaged in 1987 by the York Cemetery Trust who look after it to this day.

## Yorkshire Agricultural Society

The Society was inaugurated in 1837 by a group of agriculturalists at a meeting in *The Black Swan Hotel*, **Coney Street**. They decided that their objectives would be to establish 'an annual meeting for the exhibition of farming stock, implements, etc and for the general promotion of agriculture'. This became the Great Yorkshire Show. The first meeting was held in York in 1838 at the Barrack Yard of the 5th Dragoon Guards – so popular was it that there was a near riot at the Members' gate where soldiers and police 'were obliged to use their sticks, the blows of which were returned'. Massive sheds were built on **Bootham** Stray for the 1848 event; a specially extended branch railway was built. The 1937 show marked the centenary of the Yorkshire Agricultural Society and was held over 50 acres on the **Knavesmire**.

## The Yorkshire Museum

The Museum was founded by the **Yorkshire Philosophical Society** to display their geological and archaeological collections. It was originally in Ousegate until 1828 when the society received by royal grant, 10 acres of land from **St Mary's Abbey** in order to build a new museum. The main building was designed by William Wilkins in Greek Revival style; it was officially opened in 1830, making it one of the oldest museums in Britain. A condition of the royal grant was that the surrounding land should become a botanical garden. This was completed in the 1830s, known to us as the **Museum Gardens**. The biology collection contains 200,000 specimens, geology has over 112,500 specimens; the archaeology collection has nearly a million objects dating from around 500,000 BC to the twentieth century and includes the York Helmet (750-775), discovered in York in 1982. In 1992 the Museum paid £2.5 million for the Middleham Jewel.

## Yorkshire Philosophical Society

The Yorkshire Philosophical Society was founded in 1822 by four York gentlemen: William Salmond (1769-1838), a retired colonel and amateur geologist; Anthony Thorpe (1759-1829); James Atkinson (1759-1839), a retired surgeon and William Vernon (1789-1871), son of **Archbishop** Vernon of York, Vicar of **Bishopthorpe**. The first three met for the first minuted meeting of the Society on 7 December 1822: their aim was to collect together and house their collections of fossil bones many of which had recently been discovered at Kirkdale Cave . Vernon attended the second meeting on 14 December at which the prospectus was drawn up 'to establish at York, a philosophical society, and to form a scientific library and a museum.' Such was the genesis of the **Yorkshire Museum**. The Society's name comes from the days when 'natural philosopher' was the term for a scientist.

## York St John University

York St John's roots go back to 1841 when the York Diocesan Training School, for teacher education, opened in May 1841 with one pupil on the register, sixteen-year-old Edward Preston Cordukes. The Students' Union building is named after him. The college changed its name to St John's College in the late 1890s. By 1904 St John's was the largest Diocesan College in the country with 112 students. In 1916, half way through the First World War, the college was forced   to close because all the male students had gone to the front.  The building was requisitioned as a military hospital until it re-opened in 1919.  The affiliated women's college in Ripon stayed open, though, so that the women students could make clothes, bandages and splints for the soldiers at the front. Ripon and York merged to become the College of Ripon & York St John in 1974. By 2001 all taught courses moved to the York campus and the name York St John was adopted.

## York & Ripon Training College for Schoolmistresses

This college was established in 1846 in Monkgate in premises vacated by St John's College, between 1841 and 1845. The students were said to be 'mostly middle-class . . .

a great portion of time is consumed in instructing them in those elementary branches of learning which belong more properly to a National school than a training institution'. The college moved to Ripon in 1862.

## York Stone
Distinctive fine-grained sandstone quarried not in York but around Leeds, Halifax and Bradford.

## Zeppelin Raids
York, like other towns and cities endured Zeppelin raids during the First World War, the most destructive of which occurred on the night of 2 May 1916 when eighteen bombs were unleashed on the city , destroying buildings, killing nine people and injuring forty more. Details of this raid and two others in 1916 were suppressed until 1956. Zeppelin phobia increased and there were prosecutions of people not observing the blackout. In September another citizen was killed in a raid, leading to the establishment of York Patrols Committee; their controversial advice was for people to remain inside during raids; a doctor at the **Retreat** circulated a letter on worrying levels of *Zeppelinophobia*.